MW01171590

BLACK HORSES/WHITE COTTON AND RELIGION

A SERIES OF ESSAYS REFLECTING THE PERSONAL THOUGHTS OF A PROFESSIONAL ATHLETE

BLACK HORSES/WHITE COTTON AND RELIGION

A SERIES OF ESSAYS REFLECTING THE PERSONAL THOUGHTS
OF A PROFESSIONAL ATHLETE

by

ANTHONY PRIOR

STONEHOLD BOOKS

RIVERSIDE, CALIFORNIA

This is a Stonehold Books Publication

Copyright @ 2008 by Anthony Prior

All rights reserved. No part of this book may be reproduced
in whole or in part, in any form or by any means, electronic
or mechanical, including photocopying, recording or by any
information storage and retrieval system, without permission
in writing from the author.

ISBN 978-14-1-96803-7-3
Cover Design by Dave Guzman
Printed and Bound in the United States of America

This book is dedicated to my future grandchildren and great grandchildren. When you have to keep reminding people of who they are you can't move forward.

ACKNOWLEDGEMENTS

There's a place in the human body called "The Internal Celebration" where the external elements can't penetrate or affect the human spirit. Every human being that's made a spiritual contribution to the world has confessed of such a place.—AP

I must first acknowledge my God who gives me the strength to find the God in me to write from the heart and mind what I believe to be true. With all honor and respect to Him, I write about His glory and love for all mankind. Anytime you write on the subject of religion, it will ignite an emotional response from others, and if your views are not consistent with orthodox beliefs, those who you want to acknowledge may ask that you not do so. Out of respect for all you beautiful people that I do love, but disagree with, I acknowledge you anonymously. There have been many people who inspired this work. One stands out, a young dancer who read my previous work, *The Slave Side of Sunday*, and told me that one of the chapters in that work, "The Committee of Five Fishermen," inspired her to want to read all my works. She suggested that I re-write that chapter in more simplistic terminology. Because of her words, I have included a chapter in this book, "Leveling the Playing Field," that expounds on my theme in that particular chapter. I would like to give a special thanks to Eric Sutton, my teammate, comrade, and friend, with whom I first began to share my personal thoughts concerning sports, slavery, religion, and the Black athlete. It was Sunday, September 7, 2000 in Canada. I found myself driving Eric to the hospital for further evaluation after suffering a neck injury that would eventually end his career. Through all his pain and suffering I never once saw the man quit or discourage me in my pursuit of a writing career. His determination and will to push forward gave me the same determination to pursue writing. Also I must express a great appreciation for Nicole Cole, who has constantly taken the time out of her busy schedule to assist me in my pursuit, and help me develop my writing to its full potential. A very special thanks to my father, John Frank Prior, who not only raised five children, but works as a full time carpenter after retirement. His motto is, "Hard work doesn't kill people, and laziness does." During the latter part of my football career I had the golden opportunity to help him on a few projects. It was at that time I began to share with him my personal philosophy about life, sports, and spirituality, and how they relate to our humanity. With every project we finished, the closer I moved toward the God within. I have to acknowledge Professor Frederick Williams, former Adjunct Professor of African American Studies and Political Science at the University of Texas at San Antonio, for his manuscript analysis. He is an author in his own right. Finally, I would like to acknowledge all my teammates in the National Football League and the Canadian League who encouraged me to continue speaking out about some of the wrongs we must endure during our careers. They let me know that my writings will not fall on deaf ears and they appreciate what I am doing to inform them and future young players that things will not always remain the same.

FOREWARD

Once in a while a real maverick comes along and challenges established rules and institutions. Over the years these challenges have occurred in the spheres of economics, politics, religion, and social justice. Ghandi and Dr. Martin Luther Kings, Jr., are prototypes of the 20th Century mavericks. Now, as we near the end of the first decade of the 21st Century, a new contemporary maverick has surfaced. Like Ghandi and King, this young fighter is willing to take on one of the most powerful modern day institutions, and that is the National Football League. Anthony Prior, former National Football League and Canadian Football League player, has challenged the many preconceptions people have about these two leagues. In *Black Horses, White Cotton and Religion,* he lays open all the inequities, the exploitation and cruelties associated with playing professional football. He is especially critical of the exploitation of inner city athletes. The natural athleticism of the Black athlete is exploited in the same way as the natural strength of the slave. Much of this exploitation is intertwined in a web of religious and sports connections by charlatan ministers and owners, who both find Black players ideal prey.

In a brilliantly written chapter, Anthony analyses the tragedy of the Michael Vick saga. He raises the question why would such a gifted athlete be hanging around with two bit thieves and hood rats from his past, instead of bankers and investors who could assist him as he grew in his new world of fame, success, and finance? Anthony also asks the very cogent question is Vick's failure his to bear alone, or does he represent a failure of the larger society to bridge the gap from poverty to financial security. The much more provocative question is why are so many talented young Black men going to prison? With the number of young talented Blacks spending their most productive years behind bars, Anthony suggests that someday the National Football League could be replaced with the Prison Football League. The players would be allowed out of prison on Sundays to play other prison teams. That would be the extent of their freedom. This idea is based on the premise that most football fans love to watch the superior performance of the Black athlete, but resent the fame, fortune, and especially the women, who are a part of that success. Watch them on Sunday and lock them back up on Monday, would be the preferred method of dealing with the Black athlete to a large percentage of the population.

Throughout this provocative collection of essays, Anthony constantly points out to the reader that Black Americans are still trapped in the ugly vice of white exploitation and subtle racism. The system of exploitation is similar in the National Football League and the Canadian Football League. He is well qualified to make the comparison, since he played a total of eleven years in both leagues. In the essay about the Canadian Football League he compares the movement north by many Black ball players cut by their National Football League teams, as comparable to thousands of slaves who followed the North Star from slavery to freedom. However, just like slaves that reached Canada they were not free from economic exploitation, he writes the same is true for football players. Anthony's most controversial assertion in the chapter is his claim that Black ball players get caught in the allure of the white female sex trap. The latter are used by coaches and owners to keep players pacified and content. Some ball players, good enough to return to the National Football League, which is the superior league, chose to remain up north because of their white girlfriends or wives. Many players, who have retired and returned to the United States, are still paying exorbitant child support payments for children left behind in Canada.

Anthony's most controversial suggestion is his call for a ten year moratorium on sports being played in the African American communities all across this country. Exploitative coaches, fame-hungry fathers, and fortune-seeking mothers, are doing great damage to the young Black man. Anthony is calling on all Black communities to spend as much time on perfecting their children's academic skills as they do on athletics. We must begin to change the existing paradigm in Black communities across this nation. Reading and writing has to be our main concern. Educated Black men and women should begin to take the instructions given to us over one hundred years ago by the greatest 20th Century scholar and thinker, Dr. W.E.B. Dubois. Those of us who have the benefit of advanced educations have to reach back and help all our children to progress. The concept behind the Talented Tenth is still viable, but that group has to begin to live up to their responsibility to the community. We grow as a village and only when the entire village progresses. That is the message that this talented thinker leaves with us in this very provocative work.

Frederick Williams, Writer and Lecturer

TABLE OF CONTENTS

Page

Introduction: A Story Worth Telling   1

Chapter One: Moments of Truth   5

Chapter Two: Religion and the
                National Football League   30

Chapter Three: Canada, Freedom and Football   47

Chapter Four: Slavery and
                Christian Players in the NFL   56

Chapter Five: Michael Vick and the
                Prison Football League   70

Chapter Six: The Purchase (Fort Jesus)   81

Chapter Seven: The Ship of Zion   95

Chapter Eight: Leveling the Playing Field   111

Chapter Nine: The Philosophy of Athletics   133

Chapter Ten: In Search of a New Humanity   146

INTRODUCTION:

A STORY WORTH TELLING

"The way you start off determines how you finish." —AP

    I find myself putting on my uniform for another battle. Its game day in the Canadian Football League and the stadium is packed with screaming fans who will cheer us on to defeat the opposition. We are the gladiators of the 20th century, something all athletes dream of being, and I should be pumped, happy, thrilled to be a part of this spectacle. But my mind is elsewhere. I no longer hear the crowd as they welcome our return to the field. I run next to my teammates but wonder why I rush out here to participate in this madness. Why this time and this place in history? More importantly why am I doing this? A Black American living and working in Canada, for the pleasure of the white fans and the white owners. How did I manage to get here? Was it deliberate and planned? Maybe I have and always will be a tool for the greed, and enjoyment of others. Is this my fate or is my destiny in my own hands?

    Suddenly I have this strong urge to run back through the tunnel and into the locker room, blocking out all the sounds. I want to escape back into myself and try to search once again for my own identity, something I do quite

INTRODUCTION

often lately. The announcer is now calling the names for the starting line-up and I can anticipate the cheers when he says "starting at corner back, Anthony Prior." At this particular moment of glory my mind escapes back into the locker room and I am thinking of God. He will give you answers you can't find in books written by mortal men. Vision comes from God, the ultimate source of power and our being. He tells me that each step I've taken in this life has been an extension of my history. Just as I will run out on this field, I have been walking and running for thousands of years.

I've taken steps in Africa with the "Mali Dynasty," and during the middle ages I sat in the "city of wisdom" at Timbuktu. I ran with Hannibal, the African warrior of Carthage. We marched up the Alps and defeated the Roman army, the most powerful the world had ever known. I spoke with the wisest man of the ancient east, Lokman, whose wisdom surpasses that of Solomon in the Christian-Jewish world. Mohammed named the thirty-first chapter of the Koran after him. I have walked in chains under the control of Roman authorities, and watched as the Greek amphitheater was cleared out and my brothers from Africa fought lions and tigers to the pleasure of thousands of bloodthirsty citizens. The bloodshed and violence was praised and cheered just as we are cheer today on NFL Sunday as we prepare to do battle with other men who should be our friends, but are considered our enemies for the purpose of sport.

They are only two players away from announcing my name and I begin to prance like an animal preparing to pounce on its prey. But my mind still can't get ready for this game because it is determined to keep me on this journey of reflections to another time. I find myself in chains from neck to feet. My family is boarding ships, built by Europeans exploring new lands in order to build new European empires on the backs of my people who are hung and whipped in America, but do not die. These capitalists, who are now the modern day owners of the CFL and the NFL, and the majority of fans, are determined to break my will to be free. But I will not concede my manhood to them. I will not become their subject, their house nigger. I will leave that role to others.

I sat with Harriett Tubman and discovered the Underground Railroad, where brave and strong Black warriors helped their fellow Black brothers and sisters to freedom. I ran on the football field with Charles W. Follis in 1902, making him the first Black professional football player better known as the "Black Cyclone." I walked on the field with Gordon Simpson, the first Black Canadian football player and hear the fans scream at him, "nigger go home." I witnessed Johnny Bright, who was the NFL's overall first pick in the draft refused to play in America because of racism. Instead he abandoned his so-called homeland and played in Canada becoming the first National Football League first-round pick ever to do so. He became one of the CFL's greatest players.

It is about that time, game time. My name is next. I will go out there and participate in one of the most violent sports man has ever created. But I have been the recipient of violence for many centuries; it has become a way of life, this physical force that has been placed in my path.

"And now at right corner back, from Washington

State, Anthony Prior."

It is done. As I raise my head and put on the helmet, my eyes are fixed on the crowd as they roar approval, chills go up and down my spine. This new millennium, this new land is a place I have visited before, only under different conditions and circumstances. I reach the center of the field and my adrenaline is on fire. I hug my team mates, we exchange body slams, make guttural sounds and prepare to do battle. Regardless of the outcome the one common denominator that connects us all, both teams, the owners, the crowd, and the millions watching on television is that we have done this before in much the same way, shape, and form.

Chapter One

MOMENTS OF TRUTH

"Stop looking for God outside of yourself. The world does not need a savior. For thousands of years we have been indoctrinated to look for God outside ourselves. It is time to look within."—AP

It is a Sunday morning in December 1978, about eight minutes before ten. There is a light drizzle left over from last night's heavy rain, typical of the winter weather in Riverside, California. Church starts at ten o'clock and because we are going to be late, something also typical in Riverside, that is, the Prior family late for church, mother is irritable. She rushes my brothers and sisters, Joseph, Stanley, Stacy, Simone, and me out of the house and into our green wood-paneled station wagon. We all jump in, my siblings in the back, and because I am the youngest I jump in the front seat. We don't bother to put on safety belts because like all young kids we feel invulnerable. Our only concern is to get to church, listen to another of Reverend's fiery sermons on salvation and the love of Jesus being the only way, and hurry back home so we can do things that young people find more interesting.

As soon as we pull off my mom begins fussing, "that damn Frank hasn't fixed this windshield wiper yet." The wiper on the driver's side won't budge from the middle of the window. She has to squint to see. Mother turns the dial to the gospel station on the radio, but can barely hear Mahalia Jackson's beautiful voice singing "His Eye's are on the Sparrow." We can barely hear the music because Joseph and Stacey are making so much noise in the back seat, fussing and verbally insulting each other. "Shut up," mother scowls. She brakes at a red light, turns around to face them and spews some additional words to straighten out their behavior. Sitting up front I feel that I am exempt from her scorn, but she turns and fires away, "I don't want no mess from you in the church, either."

Mother pulls into the church parking lot; we pile out of the station wagon and hurry inside. As always, the service has begun and we've missed a few opening hymns and church announcements. The same usher who greets us every Sunday morning raises an eyebrow and gives us a church bulletin. As the song ends and the choir sits down, the sanctuary doors open and all heads turn to the back to see who is late. I can read their thoughts. "Yeah, here come the Priors." We always sit near the back on the left because those seats are reserved for members that arrive late, and yes, we are always late, but we are never absent.

Every Sunday our seating arrangement is pretty much the same. My mom, Joseph and Stacey sit in the pews directly behind me. My sister Simone would sit to my left and I always sat next to Stanley, who would sit next to the aisle. Five minutes after sitting down, Stanley would lean his head to the right and go to sleep. Mother would

6

reach up front and smack him on the head and I would even give him a nudge or two. My nudges were out of concern for the much harder blows inflicted by our mother. Once he even snored and we chuckled out loud and heard about our misbehavior from mother after church.

Stacey and Joseph were the two most bored with church service, especially if Rev would go on for a long time. Stanley and I didn't get bored because we had our own entertainment, a game called Last Lick. We would hit each other lightly, almost with just a touch. If you couldn't feel the blow, you would lose the game.

I often saw mother cry in church. Sometimes the choir would sing a hymn from her childhood or the Rev would preach or say words as if they were coming from her father's mouth. The strange thing was that whenever I saw my mother cry, I would start crying also. Whenever she felt something that grabbed her emotions, I would immediately look elsewhere. If I looked at the tears in her eyes, feelings deep in me would get all worked up and the water would pour out of my eyes. I believe those tears were my first moment of understanding the compassion God put in my heart. Those were my most intimate moments with God during my youth. I didn't really listen to Rev's words, but took my cue from my mother. When she cried I knew old Rev had said something personal that touched her and I would share that with her. When I reached high school, however, I did begin to listen. It was a time when I was uncertain of my future and that frightened me. I prayed all the time that God would deliver a football scholarship to me. He did.

Once I entered the University I lost my spiritual

path. I once got so drunk I started crying because I just knew I was going to die if I went to sleep. That night I walked myself sober and made a deal with God. I said loudly, "God if you let me live I'll never drink again, and I'll go to church in the morning. I kept my promise and the next morning I did go to church. But as I walked into the sanctuary I saw a picture of the blond-haired, blue-eyed Jesus instead of the Black Jesus we had at Allen Chapel back home. The next night I was drinking again. I rationalized my behavior thinking Jesus drank wine, so I guess a little beer in moderation would not hurt. Well, it did, and soon I was back in the same situation, too drunk to have fun, too scared to sleep, and again walking all night to sober up. I was wrestling with God and just as Jacob did in the Bible I was trying to fit God into my plans, looking for ways for Him to adapt to my thinking and my way of living. I was setting myself up for failure.

Playing Division One college football and always surrounded by a large contingent of young ladies to date, should have been prime time for me. To the contrary, I was experiencing a confused state of mind at this point in life. My girlfriend was pregnant, I was on academic probation, and they were kicking me out of my dormitory for numerous noise violations. One night, quite depressed and despondent, I called my mom. Her words were Heaven-sent. She said, "Anthony, my son, what you do in the dark will always come to the light. We all have to reap what we sow. It may not come right away, but eventually it will catch up to you. If not you, it shall fall on your children." Her words were harsh, but I needed to hear them from her. She made me realize that no matter how dark the road and how nasty the storm, God is always there with you to see you through. That conversation put everything into perspective and I got off academic probation and straightened up my life. The University decided to let me stay in the dormitory and once again my girlfriend and I were on talking terms, trying to make this all work out for the best. Not long after I thought I had worked all this out, I found myself questioning exactly where God fit in all my confusion and drama.

I constantly had to reconstruct mother's words and the manner in which they revealed a spiritual truth to me. In the midst of confusion God was right there. It would be wonderful if I could gather all the great moments with God, take each positive experience with Him and connect them into a continuum through history. My growing interest in spirituality triggered an interest in philosophy. I enrolled in a few philosophy classes. I was particularly impressed by one of my professors, who explained life in relation to two circles, the circle of influence and the circle of concern. He referred me to Stephen R. Covey's book, *The Seven Habits of Highly Effective People: Powerful Lessons in Personal Change.* The professor explained that if you choose to live in the circle of influence, you will find yourself inspired and enthusiastic because the circle of influence is a positive lifestyle. On the other hand, the circle of concern is a place of stress and confusion and the only end is self-destruction. I was enthralled by his words. I felt more powerful and for some reason closer to the meaning of life after listening to his lectures. During college, no matter how bad I messed up or how good I did on the football field, I had a message from God that the closer my relationship with Him, the better person I am, and the better player I would be on the field. I have struggled with that for years, the fact that my failure on and off the field was just another indication that my life wasn't lined up with God. Finally, one evening while out under the moon and feeling closer to our Creator, I fell on my knees and asked Him to give me only those words of truth that He wanted me to put on paper. That is what I am doing now, and I am confident that He does approve.

GAME DAY:

On game day, whether in high school, college, or professional football, my routine has always been the same. I put on some good oldies music, clean up my space at home, wash all my clothes, vacuum, and do the dishes. I even take time to pay my outstanding bills.

When I was playing for the Calgary Stampeders in Canada, one particular game day stands out and always comes back to me so clearly like it just happened. I have kept my memories and thoughts about that game to myself until now. I can still hear the chatter in the locker room. I can still feel the intensity. The locker room looks like lunchtime on a New York afternoon, with players scrambling for equipment while the equipment manager runs around frantically making sure everything is correct. Players always need something and coaches are looking for certain players to make sure they know their assignment. Some players listen to their Walkman radios and you can hear the music from their earphones because they blast it out. Other players are sleeping, some tell jokes, and the player I dislike most is the one that says, "Don't get scared now." He was always the one truly afraid.

Then there is the preacher man, the Christian player who seems to be more of a Christian than anyone else because he is holding his Bible and reading it. A group of players who believe in Jesus always gather before each game and pray. They pray for protection over their bodies. They pray for victory in the end. They even pray for the other team's safety to limit serious injury. Just before they say "amen" in unison, they hold each other's hands a little tighter to let the one next to them know that they sincerely have trust and faith in their prayer. Afterwards, there is a sense of strength and the will to be courageous in the name of God. I recall in a game one of the players who always led the prayer broke his leg right in front of me. He later said, "It was God's will, His way of slowing me down so that I can learn to lean on Him even more than I have in the past." His words rang in my head for hours after I left him.

That night, with his words still clear in my mind, I found myself again wrestling with God. I lay in bed and thoughts begin to come to me in humble ways. I begin to retrace my athletic career and God began to reveal not just moments of understanding, but also moments that have confused me. I visualize teammates preparing to go on the field of battle. They all pray for victory knowing full well that only one team can win the Championship and carry the trophy. No matter what the sport—track, boxing, baseball, or football, before most events large number of players bow their head and pray to God for victory. Each team prays that God will deliver a victory for them. Following the game, newscasters show highlights of players scoring touchdowns and raising their hands to the Heavens, saying,

"Thank you God, for blessing me and answering my prayer to score a touchdown, make a key interception, sack the quarterback, or kick the winning field goal. Thank you God for embarrassing the man on the other side of the field, who by the way, also believes in you."

The point that most players seem to miss is that you cannot glorify God on the misfortunes of other players, who also believe in and pray to the same God. When we are on the field of play, we choose to engage in the sport of our choice. Why do we pray to God for protection when we made the conscious decision to put our bodies in harm's way? Why do we pray for protection when the human body is not meant to play such a brutal game? The driving force behind our unnatural desire to participate in a game that can injure or even kill us is because of the money, fame, prestige, and time in the spotlight. When a player does magnificent feats on the playing field, the crowd roars his name, not the name of God. But God roars your name when you help somebody, feed somebody, and clothe somebody.

I often have lingering thoughts regarding what separates today's athletes and great warriors in the Bible. It seems the difference is that Biblical men such as Joshua and David had the courage to obey God, despite the disapproval of others. More important, the men of the Bible were instructed by God to fight battles for His glory alone. We athletes are instructed by our trainers and our coaches, some of whom are atheists, to execute plays they've drawn up on a blackboard that often don't work. Why do we think God is out on the field of play? It is because we often believe that when we score touchdowns, dunk basketballs, or even hit home runs, we are bringing glory to God's name. Actually, we are only deceiving ourselves from the real truth, which is that we are often seeking personal glory.

The prophets in the Bible were mighty warriors; soldiers appointed by God. They were willing to give their lives to glorify Him. These men were not playing a game. They were the real warriors of God.

Different Day, Same Tricks:

After Nat Turner's slave uprising in 1831, religion began to play a major role in the lives of the slaves and often the plantation owners would allow them to conduct controlled worship services, not for the purpose of saving their souls, but to prevent another bloody uprising. "Give them Jesus to keep them obedient," the slave owners said. "Put a Bible in their hand. Brainwash them, then we can go on with the slave trade." A Bible to prevent an uprising! The Virginia Assembly enacted new regulations that stated, " No slave, free negro or mulatto, whether he shall have been ordained or licensed, or otherwise, shall hereafter undertake to preach, exhort, or conduct, or hold any assembly or meeting, for religious or other purposes, either in the day time, or at night, under a penalty of not more than thirty-nine lashes." Whites, however, were allowed to take Negroes to their own services, and a licensed white preacher was permitted to address Negroes during the daytime. The slaves were especially taught that they would be denied to seek forgiveness if they did harm to a white person. "If any Negro should commit an assault on a white person with intent to kill, death without benefit of clergy was to be his punishment" (Herbert Aptheker, American Slave Revolt: New York, International publishers, 1943, page 314).

Unfortunately I have known athletes to use this same kind of religious abuse to gain unsupervised control of a woman. They get religious, but only for the sake of winning her over and controlling her behavior. This is quite possibly the worst and most blatant misuse of Christianity in form of manipulation. Before leaving for an out of state game, these manipulators force a Bible into their wife or girlfriend's hand in an attempt to ease their insecurities, believing it will keep her sanctified while they are gone. Knowing that this abuse occurs makes me want to scream, "You have flipped the script, my Brother. Your sincerity is as weak as your game on the field." You are allowing the beauty of her flesh and the lust in your heart to deceive you into an act of deception that someday you will regret." Proverbs 6: 24-25 tells us, "Do not lust in your heart after her beauty or let her captivate you with her eyes. For the prostitute reduces you to a loaf of bread, and the adulteress preys upon your very life."

We put the burden of our insecurities on our women. All our anxiety and emotional strain have been placed on her shoulders. Our dishonorable actions and lies awaken an overpowering spirit of destruction, yet we think we "have it going on." On the contrary, the negative things we instill in other people, especially in women, will visit us and camp out on our shoulders. All the things we have done to soothe that spirit of confusion and emotional strain will sit on us so powerfully that we will become insane, distrusting our own understanding, which leads to more foolishness.

I find it quite amusing how often I have seen the anxiety in the eyes of so many ball players when it comes to their wives, girlfriends, and significant others. I've asked the Highest about motives behind all the hype: fancy cars, expensive suits, and watches so expensive they cost more than the average monthly mortgage of the everyday citizen. These men will never be at peace with women until they learn the true beauty of the female which is her ability to express her spirituality without condemning others. A woman can make players go beyond their expectations and do extra ordinary things, and that same woman has the power to encourage a man to fight a war within him. That is why some men believe women are destroying the world, because they can trigger the worst emotions of a man making him act in such a way he would sell his soul for a woman's beauty and a nice ass. A man will spend his whole paycheck just for a little time with a beautiful woman. He stabs his best friend in the back just to lie with her. Players will knowingly take a woman out of her environment just because she is so fine and will look good on his arm while they are basking in their new found freedom in the NFL. They must learn that she will just be herself in this new environment. Even though people find themselves in a new environment, they will constantly reflect and remember who they really are in times of boredom we always reminisce. You may lead her to a new way of life, but the thoughts of old remain. She is still the same person. Often times we forget who we really are and where we belong because money brings new friends and puts us in unfamiliar circumstances.

That is why all these players, Black and white, put Bibles in their women's hands, trying to keep them pure. The truth remains that those players have slept with every woman known to them in an attempt to "sow their wild oats." When players are out of town, they make their women go to church in a hopeless effort to feel secure in their relationship. They hope the preacher will turn her mind away from the lust and temptation of sexuality and fill her mind with the judgment of God. These players' motives are fraudulent. We all know who they are. They are easily recognized. They leave the meeting room frequently to call their women, asking her questions they don't really need to ask, counting on her reading God's word to stay sanctified in order to alleviate their own fears and insecurities.

MOTIVES & MOTIVATION:

I often wonder why we do the things we do. I believe it's all about people's motives, no matter if they are an elite athlete or just associated with one, because there is a reason behind every action. Whenever I contemplate such thoughts, I pray to the God within myself to communicate with the Spirit .With the direct connection of the Spirit I can expand my understanding, in order to instinctively heighten the insight of myself and the motives of people around me. I often look at the moon in a peaceful state of mind and wait to hear from God. It is at these precious moments that God lets us know He is with us through our difficulties and He will help us to sort out the mass confusion that is loose within our soul today. We complicate our own lives and then, when things are not going well, we call upon the name of God as if He is our personal lucky charm, there at our behest to bring us good fortune and relieve us from a negative situation. I never blame God for my misfortune or pray for wealth or riches. If all we need do is pray, God would not give us free will to attain these things.

Moments with God are not limited to just a feeling or change of our circumstances. Our thoughts, concerns, and the power to articulate them are powerful, because then we can share those insights with others. Some people, athletes among them, never share their thoughts and I'm sure that most athletes have amazing and powerful thoughts. God doesn't want us to hold His knowledge when He inspires us to say something. If you are going to preach, preach the whole truth, and not just what fits comfortably into your lifestyle. Many people have countless distractions going on in their lives. They have too many people telling them too many things. What people need today is a message that puts them in control of their lives. We control our lives when we recognize that God is not at a distance rather in every breathe we take. When we start living knowing God is within us, our thoughts alone change our lives we no longer have to wait for 10 years to have a prayer answered when all we have is 10 seconds to live. Life is not meant to wait on the essentials. God did not design life to be a burden rather a constant celebration of control with our thoughts and actions. People do not have the time to hear God's words for themselves because we have been taught to look for God in other people, places, circumstances, situations, and not ourselves. Sometimes busy people have moments with God and do not even know

17

what they experienced, because of the distractions in their everyday life.

I have the ability to recognize when God is trying to tell me something. The clearest vision I ever received from the Spirit was in August 1999, the same year I did not play organized football. I was not working and my phone did not ring that much considering teams were not interested in my services. Essentially, I was not going through the stress that comes during the football season. I had no film to study, no coaches to impress, nothing to prove to my teammates. Most important, I was in a state of consciousness that the Spirit of God could communicate with little or no distractions. I was able to be still and focused with a clear mind. The Spirit communicated and gave me awareness of my surroundings .That day summed it all up, my environment and everything in my life that was good and bad was a state of mind. The Spirit spoke volumes to me I just never thought I would write about it.

It was a gray September morning and I did my usual go-on-a-little-jog-and-lift-some-weights, a routine that has become a way of life, all the while wondering about life and the chaos going on in the world. I ran a few errands and called my friend Steve and said, "Let's go see a movie tonight." I told him to pick the movie, then I plopped down on the couch and turned on the television (sometimes I call it "Hell-vision"). With the remote in my hand, I channel surfed until I finally concluded nothing was worth watching. Instead of forcing myself to watch something not worth my time, I got up and walked over to my prayer closet. I went inside and closed the door, isolating the superficial world from the real world of God's existence. I sat in my meditative position and prayed for understanding and wisdom. After a good fifteen minutes of meditation I returned to the couch, laid down and drifted off to sleep.

I found myself in another time and place. Miles and miles of cotton fields surrounded me and behind me, not too far away, I saw a church. It seemed to come toward me because my mind wanted that and I had a clear view of it. It was a white church, with five windows on the right and seven on the left. It had double wooden doors, a steeple, and a cross on top. As I cautiously walked up to the church, I wondered where the people were. Maybe inside, but when I opened the door the church was empty. It had old wooden benches lined up side by side as pews. In the center an aisle led to the altar and the pulpit. Above the altar hung a picture of a blond-haired, blue-eyed man, with his arms stretched out wide. I guess it was supposed to be Jesus. The walls were dirty and full of holes. As I looked up towards the ceiling, to my right I saw a ladder leaning next to a window, leading up to the roof. I stepped outside the window, climbed up the ladder and sat on top of the roof providing me with a clear view all around the church. The cotton fields had turned to snow, the sun had turned blue, and the sky pitch black.

Looking back into the church through a hole in the roof, I saw slaves coming in through the front door. They looked tired and hungry. Some just lay on the benches, some sat on the floor, and others leaned against the wall. They prayed, "Lord have mercy, I don't know how much longer I can hold on in this place." Others talked of uniting against this common oppression, "This is ours. We own

19

this," they said. "For this is the only thing massa has really given us revering to Christianity. Let's keep this." The slave leading the prayer seemed to be in charge, for all the others listened to what he said. Suddenly a slave came running through the front door, breathing hard and heavily sweating like he'd just run away. "They's comin', y'all." I looked up to see who was coming and saw that the cotton fields had turned to dirt. The sky was an ugly gray. I saw a group of white men striding towards the church. Some walked faster than others. The men did not enter the church, but just stood outside staring in.

As night fell, candles lit the church inside. White men still stood in groups at each window watching the slaves inside. The slaves knew the white men were staring at them. Fear took over and they began to sing and shout the name of Jesus. Some ran down the church aisles, falling and shaking on the ground saying words they could not even pronounce. The poor wretched slaves screamed "Hallelujah," over and over again. They jumped up and down out of control as if they were possessed by demons. The white men laughed and also shouted, "Yeah, these niggers are getting the message. It's working. We're making them insane and crazy for our Christianity. They shout because they're trying to convince us of their loyalty. They scream so we can hear them. They dance so we can watch them. They fall to the ground and lie there so we can laugh at them." This went on all night. As the sun came up, the white men walked away. A slave who had been spying on the white men signaled to the slaves inside they could now come together and stop all that nonsense, which they did.

The meaning of this vision was very clear to me. We, as a people have been hoodwinked. We were taught to believe in a religion for purposes of pacifying us to be content with our oppression. Given the condition of their existence, it is understandable why our ancestors bought into this hype. What is not understandable is why we continue to do so.

MY EYES WERE NOT BLINDED:

I once had another dream. In this particular dream I stared directly into the powerful rays of the sun but my eyes were not blinded.

A silhouette of a person appeared before me as I continued to stare. He had a tall stature and a commanding presence. I just kept my focus on the silhouette without trying to anticipate a response. I waited for the energy, the spirit, this vibration to communicate something to me, for this was not an ordinary dream; this energy had come from the Sun.

This force finally spoke to me, "I understand your thoughts. Don't look for any power outside of yourself. It's up to the individual to qualify themselves in this life. This voice spoke with great clarity.

"Who are you?" I asked him.

And a great vibration began to ensue and there was voice where there was silence: "I see that you are a man of simple truths, so I will be simple with you in truthful ways. I am the highest of them all."

"If you are the Highest of them all with all answers

21

and knowledge, then why is there some much evil and destruction in this world? If you're all-powerful, why don't you end it?" My insides churned slightly talking to such a powerful force in somewhat of an obstinate tone.

The Highest of them all spread energy so tremendous with warmth I could feel it emanating from within. "If I were to get rid of all evil and death in the world, there would be no human beings, my child. It's human greed that is destroying this world of pleasure."

"Why don't you stop these human beings?" I asked.

"There are things that have to happen first my child," He answered. " Like nature there is always a cleansing process and that's what is transpiring. Iit's the transition of Good over Evil. My prophecy has to be fulfilled, and what you see in today's world is mass destruction, evil, murder, killing of brothers and sisters, of entire families." He paused to breathe in deeply and release it. "It's a natural cycle of life that has to be fulfilled. I tell you, my child it's going to get even worse. You must realize the human being has been dehumanized. There is a part of my spirit, my essence, glory, and power that dwells inside you, and every human being walking the great earth must realize they have the power to turn on this limitless power that's within ," the Highest of them all said.

"Why are the human beings suffering so much here on earth?"

Now a very serious feeling of energy spread across my presence and I could feel a sense of pressure and tension. "The dehumanization of human beings is a prophecy that needs to be fulfilled in order to bring on a better way of life that nurtures the human spirit. The

22

humans of today are a lost tribe and they have been in captivity for many centuries. When talking about captivity I'm referring to the captivity of their mind. The thinking of human beings has caused every tribulation in their little circle of life. Just as the human being has become unpredictable in their endeavors so have the weather patterns. The multitudes of today are people that are confused, but the human spirit who knows me will recognize my voice and see the signs as clear as day and they will not be afraid." The voice paused again and penetrated even deeper into my meditation. *"I'm not coming in the name of religion or institutions that claim to believe in the Holy Spirit, for they are as corrupt as the rest of the world. I am not coming for those who say they are Christians, Muslims, Jews, Buddhists, or any religious affiliation. They will be put on trial at the end. The day of God coming is just a phrase since I never left. Once you realize you are God also, time will stop, and your life will begin. Tell the world, my child, the higher power lives inside of the people. Turn the people on to themselves and make them turn on that switch of power to transform their life. Waiting on correction and change doesn't happen by chance it must come from within. The real sign of a man of God is that he takes care of his people by having them become independent of him, not dependent on him.* I listened as this mighty voice of reason and correction began to disappear.

"My child, you prayed to me and I have come to answer the concerns of your heart. Now realize it didn't cost you anything. I need nothing from you for I am that I am. All I ask is for the human race to love each other as I love you all collectively and individually."

I awoke and felt peace all around me. I have never told this story until now. I believed the time was right to share this vision with others. After experiencing the highest I now understand why corruption exists everywhere, even in the church. I recognize it's an institution built on material things and not on the love of God. Why is it when pastors and ministers come from a distant place to give us the word from God, first we must give them money and they have the nerve to pass around buckets and trays and proclaim, "This is God's money and you're in God's house." I don't think so. Man has built these buildings. You notice that during tax season, before you get your income tax check, pastors and ministers all over the country start talking about tithing to the church. What they are really saying is "Give me some money to help me pay for the new house I bought, the big car in my driveway." Tax season is a time when the value of the stock in some these churches rises. Pastors, just like CEO's, should have public financial records open to the members so they know exactly where the money is going.

A pastor's financial statement might read something like this: money for their children to go to private schools, while yours attend an underfunded, worn down public school, with too many students and not enough teachers and not enough books. Their children's clothes are bought from the most expensive stores in the mall while that tithing mother can hardly buy a pair of pants from Wal-Mart. What ever happened to pastors focusing on loving more than taking? When the Highest spoke in front of the multitudes He never asked for anything. People felt the need to give out of love. Now greed has become as prevalent and evil as Satan. I am not placing all ministers in the same bag, but it has been my experience that a great deal of them fit that mold. Corrupt pastors and ministers come in all shapes, sizes, colors, and creeds. They are all human just like you and me.

The highest told me, "Spend most of your time loving people. The only lasting emotion is love. Everything else will fade, my child. Love with no limits and no conditions, and I will awaken in you. On my return, all people on earth shall come to a heightened awareness and proclaim the God within them, and the old way of thinking shall perish in the fire of their own greed, deceit and destruction. Death will come to the minds of old that have their thoughts in the past and the old ways of living, thinking and believing.

The highest wants the world to take a close look at its functioning today. The churches are money making institutions now. They have conformed to the world's standard of living, thinking, and worshiping. Like the change of weather, the church has also decided to put Christmas lights around her steeple and Christmas trees in her churches. She has brought Easter bunnies into her midst; hiding eggs like Satan has hidden the truth from millions. The church has Thanksgiving feasts. She sits with savages sharing stories of greed and death, and yet they say they are not conforming to this world. These pagan rituals have caught more interest in the minds of millions who claim to be holy. We can only be holy if we possess holiness.

A new kind of holiness is also walking around athletic locker rooms; it is in the form of profiteering pastors. They prey on Black athletes, claiming God has given them a platform to spread His message. Ask a

25

Capitalistic pastor, "Where did that platform come from?" He will avoid answering you, but instead tell you how great you are and how God has destined you to do great things on the playing field to demonstrate His glory through your body. Ask that same minister about your mental capabilities, how smart you are and how you want to be remembered for what you know rather than how fast you run. Ask him why is it when you are invited to give your testimony around his congragation, he always critiques your words and tells you what to say? To add to the insult, he also tells you what not to say, so you don't make him uncomfortable. What he is saying quite clearly is, "I'll put you on that platform to be viewed as a specimen like my European ancestors did. When your ancestors came off the boats as slaves, they were put on a platform to be sold at any price and now it is my turn to take advantage of your physical prowess on a religious platform."

When you become an athlete it is as if once again the white man puts you on a platform to show off his Black Stud. He takes you to the NFL Combine and lets you walk on a platform to compare you to the other Black studs just as he has done since the birth of America. Then you come to an NFL plantation that has bought you. There, waiting for you is the profiteering pastor telling you, "I got a new plan for you to help me fill my church the way you fill a stadium. Economically I need you. You're not the average Black man on the street. He can't do shit for me, but since you're in the paper and on television, you'll bring people to my church just out of curiosity alone, to see a slave up close and personal." God does not need us to spread His word for a man. We need Him for our own salvation to elevate our moral ascension. A platform is to show off an athlete's accomplishment on the football and baseball field and the basketball court as well as on the track. It is not an opportunity for profiteering pastors to pimp Black athletes.

I had a discussion on this very topic of White pastors and Black athletes with a pastor I met in our locker room when I played for the New York Jets. He told me that I had a problem when I challenged his right to recruit Black players for his own exploitation.

"You have a real problem and you are an angry man," he said.

"But you can't win me over with your interpretation of Jesus," I retorted.

"Young man, you need Jesus. The devil has a hold of you and you must repent right now," he scowled.

The man irritated me so I continued to pursue him. "Let me ask you a question," I said. "Why is it that chapels services across the NFL are filled with Black players, far more than the whites?"

"So many of you come from broken homes you need Jesus to fall back on and many of you can't survive in structured environments you need the discipline of Christ to function in America," he quickly answered as though this was a standard response.

I deliberately laughed, "And you will be the man to give Him to us?" I asked with great sarcasm.

"Oh yes, you can accomplish so much with Him in your life," he said.

I moved closer, "Can I open your Bible?" I asked.

He gently put it in my hands as if it were about to fall apart. I opened it and saw Jesus and the prophets all painted white as snow. I handed it right back to him, looked in his eyes, and said, "All you're doing is promoting white supremacy and you should stop."

"How can you say such a thing Anthony?" He said my name as proof of his intimacy and love for me.

This man's condescending ways were annoying. "Before we can understand something, we have to get to the root of it first," I explained. "Look at our beautiful country. Slave labor helped build the White House and the Capitol, and what do you see when you are inside their walls. Picture after picture of white men you call the founding fathers. The slave labor helped build white churches as well. When you walk into those buildings, you see paintings of a man called Jesus and all his prophets. They are all white. That's why Black folks feel compelled to show great deference and respect to whites like the paintings have power or something. That same misguided spirit lives in many Black athletes as it lived in the minds of the slaves. 'I need a white man in the form of Jesus in order to worship Jesus,' they say." Our discussion abruptly ended.

He turned to walk away from me. I knew he was angry and disgusted because the native had risen up in a rebellious nature and challenged the "Massa."

I wasn't finished with him yet. I called out, "When you come into the locker room with your Bible, what I really see is a new form of white supremacy. You come in here all excited about what?" I paused for emphasis. "Putting a Black man on a platform and telling him how to dress, where and when to speak, what to say, and how to say it. You call that a testimony from God in front of your congregation? Pimps do the same thing with their prostitutes."

He now stopped and glanced back for a final dose of my knowledge.

"Get to the origin of your knowledge," I continued, now in total control. "Try reading the original Hebrew Scriptures rather than the English translation of the Bible. Get to the root, fill yourself, head to toe, with knowledge you do understand. In other words, make yourself holy." I finished and turned to walk away as he had done the same. He probably didn't understand where I was coming from, but he did realize that his game could not be run on me. For what he failed to realize is that I have meditated many times and my moments with God cannot be penetrated with weak, holier than thou nonsense that is predicated on programming me and keeping God far away from me. The tricks of old cannot stand today because people are realizing the old things of the past were never fixed by the religion of today.

Chapter Two

Religion in the National Football League

"I used to have people tell me God has given you the ability to play football so you could tell the world about Him. When *you look at Scriptures, you'll see that most of the prophets weren't popular guys. I came to the realization that what God needed from me more than anything else is a way of living instead of this thing I was saying. Now I know I've got to sit down and get it right."* Former NFL Great Reggie White.

God commanded us to have stewardship over the earth, and it is our duty to conduct our personal lives in a way that glorifies Him. Playing football is an unnatural act that can bring serious injury and sometimes death to the human body, which is the temple housing the spirit of God within us. To say I love God and then destroy my body is a contradiction to the law of God. Why build your body up only to tear it down? *2Corinthians 6 verse 16* tells us, "what agreement hath the temple of God with idols? for ye are the temple of the living God; as God hath said, I will dwell in them, and walk in them; and I will be their God, and they shall be my people."

I played professional football for eleven years and have come to realize over that long time period that God does not care about football, men do. The human body was not designed to play such a violent game; it breeds satanic characteristics such as envy, jealousy, physical destruction, and chaos. These traits go against a loving God of the universe, who embraces love and not confusion. Spiritualists say God is everywhere. He is in the wind, the water, and the fire. God is someone you cannot escape; you continuously experience His divine essence. I agree that God is everywhere, however, the God of love and peace is not in every action.

God's action is not in slavery.

God's action is not in war

God's action is not in racism

God's action is not in crime

God's action is not in football

God's action is not in favoritism

God's action is not in hatred

God's action is not intimidation

God's action is not in inequity

God's action is not in killing

I would argue that the above dictums are the property of the devil. He has power over the above listed activities because human beings have replaced their God given humanity for material gains within a very secularly controlled world. When Christian football players have this notion that God loves them enough to allow them to beat up on their competition, they have lost focus of the meaning of love and accepted in its place confusion. Putting the Creator in a position to choose one player over another, one athlete over the other, is symptomatic of our human flaws. This corruption has affected every nation, state, city, and family. Man has forgotten or ignores *Acts 10 verse 34* when we are instructed, "Then Peter opened his mouth and said, of a truth I perceive that God is no respecter of persons."

We have forgotten that God gave us free choice, free will, and freedom to shape our life to our choosing. When a football player chooses to put on the uniform, place the helmet on his head, and engage in this physically barbaric sport in front of 80,000 screaming fans and millions of television viewers world-wide, he's putting himself in a hellish situation. This is not ordained by God, but to the contrary goes against His desires for us to live in peace and love. There is nothing peaceful about football and you might love your fellow player off the field, but during the game it is war. Every player must consider the following possibilities when stepping into the arena:

I could be killed

I could be paralyzed

BLACK HORSES/WHITE COTTON AND RELIGION

I could be embarrassed

I could be defeated

I could be eliminated

I could be violated

What the fans never know is that the fearless players on the field actually go into what I call "survival mode" once the whistle blows and the ball sails through the air at the beginning of the game. Understand during practice all week long players psyche themselves up for the sixty minutes of battle on Sunday. The confidence they have built up during the week of practice dissipates with the first sound of helmets clashing and bodies flying through the air. After each play the gladiators on the field breathe a sigh of relief that they are still in one piece with no bones sticking out of place or no concussions causing severe headaches. It is at this point of survival that religion and the football player part company. To bring the Living God of peace and admiration into this barbaric action would take away the intensity of the player and weaken him to his opponent. It is a blatant contradiction to concentrate on God while trying to annihilate your opponent without feelings of guilt for hurting and, on rare occasions, crippling the other person. In order to spread the gospel of love, which is the duty of the believer, I must have a peaceful mind, be in a peaceful place, expressing myself in a peaceful manner, because that is God's energy.

Why do players sacrifice their love of God on

Sunday afternoon? It is the love of money, prestige and fame that causes us to go out there and jeopardize our physical and mental well being for sixty minutes. Many players understand what they are doing is wrong and goes against the teachings in the Bible. They are playing the role of modern day gladiator much in the same image as the gladiators of old. But at the end of the game many of us will kneel and pray, often with players from the other team, thanking God for bringing us through the battle so we are ready for another day. On the field we ignore the fact that God is not in every action and this is sixty minutes of action in which He is not there. It is sixty minutes given over to the Satanic powers of the evil forces that make material wealth and fame more important than love, compassion, and happiness for our fellow human beings. I believe the fans have more sense than the players because they know violence is not a characteristic approved by God. The fans want to see the violence, but never be a recipient of it. In order for me to spread the Gospel of love and peace, I must have a peaceful mind, be in a peaceful place, expressing the word of the living Savior in a peaceful manner, because that is the energy of God in which we all strive to maintain and want to remain for eternity. Football is a distraction from that goal.

Promoters of Violence:

The football fields today are being transformed into artificial fields to save costs in water and seed usage and maintenance. It is a field where no seeds of life can take root and grow. These so-called Christian coaches (more about their false Christianity later) promote the violence, which as we have well established, is not a characteristic of Christianity, or the likeness of Jesus Christ.

Wally Buno, one of the most successful coaches in the Canadian Football League and under whom I played 2 years of ball, considers himself a Christian. He claims to live his life in a manner pleasing to God. When the twin towers fell in New York City on September 11, 2001, and Islamic extremists became the new "niggas" on the hit list of Americans, Mr. Buno took the liberty of cutting a Muslim player, Fawon Zimbety, not because he was playing terribly, but because he was a Muslim. At the beginning of the 2002 season, Zimbety was number one on the depth chart for his position. He came into the season bigger, stronger, and faster than the previous year. One day, Mr. Zimbety showed up at camp with his "garb" on. He instantly went from first team to third team. Eventually, the coach told Mr. Zimbety to leave the facility, and take his religion with him. Mr. Buno believed he had a terrorist on the team. The irony of the Zimberty tragedy is that he was not a violent man off the field. His violence was perpetrated by behavior expected of him by the coach. Bruno was the promoter of violence in order to please the owner, because it was the violent action of players like Zimberty and me that filled the stadium with fans and made money for the bosses and won a Championship. These stadiums are not filled in order to bring the body of Christ to the fans. To the contrary, they are filled for economic reasons: to build the masters of capitalism's kingdom on earth. He reaches his goal through the violent actions of men who should be praising God instead of the mighty dollar. God has nothing to do with the violence or the money. *Zephoniah 1 verse* 9 reads, "In the same day also I will punish these that leap on the threshold which fill their masters' houses with violence and deceit."

When you see the coaches running out the tunnels, they are carrying the players to their destruction. God is not in the business of carrying innocent people to their crucifixion. But many of the Christian coaches brainwash players into believing they are actually building God's kingdom while destroying their bodies as well as the opposition. On some teams the coaches make prayer mandatory. This is wrong and I believe a sin against God. I say it is wrong because the coach is not concerned about the salvation of the players but only in using faith as a tool to get the players to elevate their game on the field. He must pump up his men (the players) to play with vigor and strength, and do the will of God with all his might. I once heard a coach say to his players, "Men I'm not watching you, the Lord is so give it your all for His glory, and if for some reason you don't believe you can stay your unbelieving ass in the locker room." These coaches are so misguided they promote violence, bloodshed, greed, hatred, jealousy, envy, punishment, fear, and yes, sometimes death. Finally, in the coach's mind all players "are anathema to him," a dead man walking with no emotions, no connection to God, only the one the coach can show him. As long as the coach detaches his emotional feelings from the players, it is easy to lead them to slaughter because in his eyes the player is nothing but a sacrifice to help him reach his goal. He will keep you around and praise you as long as you keep running for his glory and not for the glory of the Lord.

I always found it ironic as a pro football player when the entire team would pray and moments later we would send out our team captains to the fifty yard line. Our opponents would send out their captains as well and a declaration of war was agreed upon, the game would begin, and our prayers were in the wind. Realize, whether in life or in sport, you can have a team that is far superior than its opponents, however, the weaker team can appear as mighty as long as the coaches from the press box above call the right plays for the weaker team. As long as I know what you are going to do before you do it, I'll beat you every time. Football players are not paid to think on the football field, they are paid to react in a split second. I once saw my defensive coordinator and the offensive coordinator of our opponent having dinner the night before the game. They both had note pads in their hands and were busy taking notes. The next day during the game, we were in the fourth quarter defending the goal line. Our coach called a cover 2 defensive play, basically, giving them a touchdown if we had obeyed his call. As players we changed the call in the huddle, stopped them from scoring and would you believe, the coach was angry with us. You would think he would be elated because we stopped the opponent from scoring or just maybe our coach had an ulterior motive.

Sustainability:

Even though most players will join in for prayer not all of them are men of religion. After 11 years of bowing my head with Christians, Muslims, Jews, Mormons, Seventh-day Adventists, Jehovah Witnesses, Buddhists, and even atheists, I came to realize that approximately 3% are true to the faith, and when their lives seem to be in harmony with God's will and the sun is shining favorably on the player that number jumps to about 5%. Other than that, players use the title Christian Athlete for one purpose only, and that is sustainability. Many players attend Bible study, or chapel service only as a gesture to fit in as a team player and to avoid criticism.

Sustainability is the art of keeping something going over a considerable time period. Players will often mock the Chaplain after a study session, saying such things as "who in the hell does he think he is, my master? How can he preach peace and brotherhood? Just look at this world; we are at war people are starving and dying because there is no food and often they must drink polluted water. Racism, sexism, and hatred exist in this world and we're actually praying to God to ask for a favor to play a child's game, and do what the body was never meant to do."

As I reflect back over my life, I must ask myself have my prayers really been answered. My entire life I have visualized and meditated on making it to the National Football League and I made it. Should I thank God for delivering on those prayers or do I question why he would answer prayers that put me in a position to be seriously injured and possibly killed? Is the chapel service for my benefit, considering I would be only hours away from going to battle on the football field, where Christians and other religious folks carry on a barbaric, unnatural activity called a football game? Is it the will of God for any of us to be:

A football player

BLACK HORSES/WHITE COTTON AND RELIGION

A boxer

An ultimate fighter

A slave

A soldier

A hit man

A liar

Every athlete and all others also will have that moment in their life when things change, sometimes for their favor and for the benefit of others. In 1977 the country watched a strong and powerful Black man named Herb Lusk run down the football field on his way to the end zone and another touchdown. On this particular Sunday, Herb Lusk believed God was granting him divine favor over his opponent and when Mr. Lusk crossed the white line of the end zone he kneeled and prayed to the God of Heaven and Earth thanking him for Glory. This was the public display of faith in the NFL on national television and Herb Lusk became a marked man. Whenever Herb would score he would fall to his knees, hold his arms in the air, and give tribute to God for allowing him to again achieve victory, and his actions escalated throughout the sports world with many Christian athletes displaying their faith publicly. He was the first professional football player to interject that ritual into the game. Herb essentially opened the door for organizations to jump on the band wagon and further incorporate religion into the game. "Athletes in Action" actually gained access to the locker room before and after the games. Chaplains, ministers, and all persuasion of religious leaders from all over the country joined the band wagon. I remember one very slick minister who flew in from somewhere in Tennessee on Monday evening to meet with the Christian Players on Tuesday evening. To this day I do not believe it was coincidence that he picked the day to show up at our facility when we collectively deposited approximately 3 million dollars in pay into our checking accounts. I was one of the only players that resented this intrusion into our lives by a man we knew very little about. We all gathered in the training room and he moved to the front of the group.

"Men, I'm here as a representative of God and He has spoken to me, asking that we all in this room give 10% of our earnings to help build His kingdom on earth, and bring peace to all mankind."

I could have lost it right there, but I maintained my composure as this charlatan, dressed in a blue suit, white shirt, and yellow tie just like he was out of the back woods of Tennessee, conned players out of their earnings. I looked around the room where about 25 of us had gathered to listen to this man who claimed to represent the Lord. I did a quick calculation in my head, and if every player actually gave this con artist 10% of their weekly earnings he would have walked out of there with about 1.2 million dollars. In my mind I was thinking I'll give you 10% when you have...

Trained like me and shared muscles aching with me

BLACK HORSES/WHITE COTTON AND RELIGION

Suffered like me as a 250 pound fullback headed directly at me with full steam ahead and no help from the linebackers or safeties.

Prayed like me when I wasn't sure I would get up to play another down

Lived like me as a Black man in a America

Have similar history like me whose roots have been built around oppression

Have experienced no justice, equality, and little freedom in the land of the free.

I could clearly discern the contradiction if I were to give this con artist 10% of my Black earnings so that he could take it back into a community that ignores the plight of my people trapped in the hell hole inner cities of America. These large religious organizations (which often include the Black churches) are not interested in the Black community and its economic development. The most many of them will do is give a free turkey at Thanksgiving and a ham at Christmas. People need jobs as well as full stomachs. These ministers who show up at our facility are there and not on the streets of Harlem, Detroit, Chicago, or St. Louis because there is no mega bucks for them to rip off in those places. This man showed up on a Tuesday evening under the guise of spreading the word to us about salvation. And parenthetically, his message of salvation was directly linked to tithing, which is true with too many of these rip off

41

artists of all races. Our visiting minister continued on his mission with most men attentively listening to his every word.

" Now you men, who have been blessed with an outstanding talent, given to you by our Lord and Savior Jesus Christ and our father in Heaven, expects you to use your talent to spread the word of God both on and off the field of play." He paused for effect and also to see if any of his pawns had pulled out their check books. No one had yet given any indications they were going into their wallets for his profits so he continued. "You must be true to the Scriptures that instruct us to not cheat our Father of His share of our earnings. After all, look what he has done for you all. You could still be stuck in the doldrums of the ghetto, living a lower class life. Instead you are well paid heroes living the life you chose. Don't you feel you owe our Lord something for rewarding you in such a fulfilling manner?"

Suddenly, a number of my team mates pulled out their check books and began to write a check to this con man. I wanted to jump up and scream, "No, don't you dare fall for this scam. You don't owe this man anything but a swift kick in the ass and a toss out of our private quarters which he has invaded bringing a false teaching of God. No, my brothers, you don't have to equate a game filled with violence and sometimes death with your relationship to God. He doesn't need you to preach His word in the middle of this battle. He seeks a different venue for His word to be spread. I would shout at them from *Psalms 7 verse 14,* "Behold, he travelith with iniquity and hath conceived mischief, and brought forth falsehood."

Just imagine the amount of money a member of the clergy can claim when in the locker room with naïve young men who only understand the scriptures found in *Ephesians 6 verse 5-8,* "Slaves obey your earthly masters with respect and fear, and with sincerity of the heart, just as you would obey Christ. Obey them not only to win their favor when their eye is on you, but like Slaves of Christ, doing the will of God from your heart. Serve whole –heartedly as if you were serving the Lord, not men. Because you know that the Lord will reward everyone for whatever good he does, whether he is slave or free."

Imagine how a fake prophet can use this scripture for his personal and financial gain. God does not need your money; he needs people to follow Him from the goodness of their heart. If a preacher, Chaplain, minister, or any religious leader asks people to give money to build the Kingdom of Heaven, he is being disingenuous or has a mental problem. Before man ever set foot on the face of the earth, God had already built, constructed, completed, finished, and consummated the heavens and earth. For men of the cloth to have the audacity to claim that God needs our tithes to finish His work is outrageous. They are arguing that God's Kingdom is not already complete and the 10% from man will go a long way in helping Him to do what is already done. Today, we have educated grown men tearing down heaven in order to increase their personal business operations, both in numbers and dollars.

ESPN "Outside the Lines"

As a guest on ESPN's Outside the Lines in December

2007, I was given the opportunity to share some of my thoughts regarding religion, slavery, and the National Football League. After the show, I was inundated with e-mails from fans, some inquisitive and others infuriated. Many fans asked if I was a Christian or an atheist. I responded to them that Anthony Prior is a true believer of the God who created the universe, who strategically placed every star in the heavens, put the moon, sun, and earth in a constant motion of harmony and not on a crash course to destroy humanity. You do not need objective scientific analysis to understand the balance between the sun, moon and earth. To the contrary, I call it God's motion and every living creature on the earth celebrates that motion. One of the host on the program, with somewhat of a smirk on his face asked, "Anthony, what do you believe?"

I pondered the question for a few seconds and smiled. "I know that I don't have to resurrect a man higher than myself to get to God," I said. "That is what I believe and my thoughts have been heard, demonstrated, manifested, and brought into fruition." I smiled at my host and added, "I prayed to God to have national exposure because I believe I have a message to deliver and I'm now on ESPN, the biggest sports network in the country. Is it an accident or luck?" I again paused. "I will let the world be the judge. I believe every man, woman, and child should judge only themselves because God never gave us the power to judge others, but if you're encouraged to give an opinion, always back it with facts, because there's only one judge who sits high and looks low."

Psalms 50 verse 6 instructs us, "And the heavens shall

44

declare his righteousness; for God is judge himself. Selah."

How should we view Herb Lusk's actions back in 1977? Is he a hero or a villain? Does God only allow Christians to score touchdowns, or does he give a pass to the atheist from time to time and allow him to share in the glory. Don't laugh, atheists also score touchdowns. It was important for Herb Lusk to really believe that God intervened in those games and gave him an advantage over all the other players. It is important because he needs someone to believe in, given the turbulent life most Black players lead before they make it to the NFL. And so when the owners invite slick white preachers in blue suits and white shirts, with yellow ties to come into our privacy and interrupt us with their special version of salvation, then it is no wonder that many fall for their game. It shows the vulnerability of very tough men and trust me football players are tough. But the fact is that God is not going to take sides in such a violent sport and favor Lusk over all the players on the opposite team. More than likely he is going to remain neutral in all violent sports. I always chuckle when I watch boxers go to their corner before the beginning of a fight and do the sign of the cross or raise their outstretched arm toward Heaven as a gesture of deference and request for victory from God. As I mentioned earlier in this essay, God is everywhere, but he is not in every action. In war, in football games, in boxing matches and in all other activities that pit one human being against another God is absent. But we continue to observe an inordinate amount of religious activities within the world of sports. I tell players all the time displaying your faith on national television is not a cure for America's problems. Between

RELIGION IN THE NATIONAL FOOTBALL LEAGUE

1977 and 2007 religious sports organizations have experienced a plethora of wealth from the players. If you analyze the cities from which these players come, you will find that their communities are the worst and are the most poverty stricken in the country. So why are we doing this as professional athletes who come from the ranks of these overrun and dirty apartment buildings, dirty streets, poorly equipped schools and over crowded jails. We give in order to help build the kingdom of strangers, and they give nothing back to us. Finally, the last time I checked, Jesus was not scoring touchdowns in the Bible. To emulate Christ is not to put on a football helmet and beat another player into oblivion if that is what it takes to win. To the contrary, to be a true disciple of Christ is to help the downtrodden, teach love and, most important, to understand the concept of forgiveness which we all are instructed to do in order to someday dwell in the Kingdom of God.

Until there is a collective consciousness throughout this country to fix the problems that plague us, then conditions for a certain segment of our population will continue to worsen. Will football players ever recognize the contradictions in their actions of pointing to Heaven when they are victorious on the field? When a Muslim player scores a touchdown and prostrates, "Allah Hu Akbar, Allah Akbar, Allah Akbar, Allah Akbar, we will then witness the end of public displays of faith throughout the sports industry.

Chapter Three

CANADA, FREEDOM, AND FOOTBALL

So they answered Joshua, saying, "All that you command us we will do, and wherever you send us we will go." Joshua 1:16

Whether you are a coach or a player, everyone involved in professional football wants to be associated with the National Football League (NFL). That is especially true of individuals in the Canadian Football League (CFL). Players who are unable to cut it in the NFL will often go up to Canada to play. Players who have enjoyed a good career in the NFL but find their skills have waned to the point that their old team no longer wants them will also run up to Canada to play. I guess my point is that the CFL in no way measures up to the standards of the giant of a league in the United States. They have a long way to go before they will be able to compete south of their border.

I played seven years in the NFL and four in the CFL. I can assure you that there is no comparison between the leagues. In fact, the players from Canada look at us in awe of our talent, even at an older age. They almost consider it a privilege to play with the guys who had careers in the NFL.

CANADA, FREEDOM AND FOOTBALL

I was also shocked at the negative attitude American players have when playing in Canada. They complain about the pay (much lower than in the states), they complain about the facilities, the food and the entire Canadian way of life. What they do not complain about is the easy availability of women, especially the Black ballplayers and the white girls. Black ball players are like children in the candy shop. You would think they had never seen a white woman before in their lives. And the coaches will use those women to trap the players into staying in Canada when oftentimes they could return to the states and play. This subject will be discussed in depth at another place in this chapter.

Black ballplayers often refer to going north as following the North Star to Canada, an obvious reference to our ancestors who escaped out of slavery by following the North Star. The great Frederick Douglass named his newspaper *The North Star* as a symbol of freedom. In one of my lowest moments while in Canada I asked a Black ball player if he knew who Frederick Douglass was. He said "Is he an ex-CFL player?" He was serious. I didn't know whether to slap him or just sit him down and give him a good history lesson. I was outdone. I couldn't stop laughing and turning my head away from him in disbelief. Today, in the 21st Century, Black players in the CFL are still following the stars to Canada, to find freedom on the football field.

Sometimes a man must run for his liberty instead of waiting on the same god of his "massa" to give it to him. We ex-slaves of the 21st Century are still trying to stay alive in the cotton patch disguised as a football field to demonstrate our physical gifts. Run-away slaves would often make quilts that would contain star patterns laying out escape routes. The free slaves used their immense talents to assist their brothers and sisters still stuck in bondage but anxious to also escape to a new beginning. NFL players who can no longer cut it take the identical route to escape to their new beginning.

I followed that North Star in May 2000, after the NFL closed its door on me. Unlike my ancestors, however, those of us who make that trip don't have to sneak off in the night and run for our life. We now receive a plane ticket, sometimes first class, or take a bus with a scenic view, and at every stop have the option of a hot meal. Some of us even drive our cars, listening to our music, or talking on the cell phone, telling our friends and family how great it feels to have the opportunity to extend our careers on the football field. We, the ex-slaves of the 21st Century are still trying to stay alive in the cotton fields by running up North to find football fields and demonstrate we still have the physical gifts necessary to play the sport.

Usually when an ex-slave gets cut from the NFL he calls one of his buddies, or a former teammate, who had already run up North. He wants to know what it is like up there, and his teammate's words become his quilt; the blanket of hope, and his means of contacting CFL teams to get a chance to continue his career. I have talked with a number of very good players coming north when they had the talent to play in the United States. In those kinds of cases it was very difficult for the player (usually Black) to deal with the favoritism he had to confront with NFL coaches. A white player who may not be quite as good as someone Black will usually get the spot on the team. That is when the Black will run up to the CFL, not only to continue he career, but to prove to the NFL coach what a stupid mistake he made. History tells us many runaway slaves that made it to Canada took their unique skills back to America after the Civil War. Taking one's skills back to the NFL doesn't happen too often.

Time and age are terrible realities to an athlete who watches his skills fade away. I have witnessed this beast affect older players trying to hold onto something that just can't last. It is so sad to see a player wear out his welcome, and it is hard to give up gifts and raw talent that have carried him so long, but we all must pass the torch someday. When the administration in the NFL takes that hatchet and knocks your brains out, the first thing you do is call your agent complaining about how you were wronged. The agent listens for a while, and he's not too concerned until you start calling every ten minutes, asking him if any teams are interested in you. You get restless. Bills are piling up, the kids are going without, and your family's telling you to get a "real" job. You're desperate and your agent can hear the urgency in your voice. He then calls up Harriett Tubman asking, "Do you have enough room on this railroad to Canada? I have a restless slave getting on my nerves?" When a player does get a call from the CFL and lands a job with one of the teams, his agent is relieved, because the player now has the opportunity to play the game he loves and also has money to take care of his family. The agent is relieved because he finally got rid of that particular client's nagging and complaining. He no longer has to worry about telephone calls all times of day and sometimes late into the night. It gives new meaning to "Got this monkey off my back." Your agent has just railroaded you to the CFL.

When you finally find a place on a team up north, the coach will usually make you feel that the CFL is your last opportunity. They act as though they are your last hope to play football, just like they are doing you a favor. They do have a playbook in one hand and a whip in the other, and the fear you experienced in the NFL resurfaces in Canada. You realize that Canada has the same pressures and some of the same problems you encountered in the NFL. The scale is different but the weight is the same. When a player goes to Canada with a bad attitude, he will have a miserable career whether it lasts one year or ten. But if he follows the North Star and gets to Canada with the attitude that he's going to make it an enjoyable experience, it'll happen ten-fold. Whatever he thinks about, he shall bring about. If the player has a negative attitude about playing in Canada he will concentrate on the down side of all things around him. If he looks for racism and hatred, they will sit down next to him like they are his best friend. With that kind of attitude, he'll hate the league and also come to hate himself.

Players who attempt to return to the NFL after one year or two in the CFL often fail miserably, especially the Black players. Some white players do make the giant leap and do well back in the big leagues. It is a humbling experience when you return for a tryout with an NFL team, but fail and then have to go back to your Canadian team with head bowed. Despite your failure you still believe that your talents far exceed the level of players in the CFL. Those players find themselves running back to freedom in the CFL with their pride so shattered and humbled that they try to ignore their peers who are laughing behind their back, and happy that they failed. At that point these players hold on to the CFL like it is their very last chance at success in the world. They finally realize they have no other talents, have not concentrated on developing any kind of mental skills, and will be a failure once they have to leave the football field. Black football players spend too much time running from reality and hiding in a fantasy world where pro football has seduced their minds and paralyzed its growth.

This is best illustrated with the relationship of Black ball players and white women in Canada. To some of the ballplayers they are like a delicacy and are readily available. Some Black players feel that they have entered a world of fantasy with so much whiteness all around them. They are running from reality and the white woman temporarily provides them with a place to hide. When Black players first arrive in Canada, the coaches (usually white) make sure there are a sufficient number of white women to meet the physical and emotional needs of these players, some single and others married. It is simply another way of "dummying" down Black men. It is another tool to keep them in check, subservient and obedient to the "massa." The irony is that the coach will use the sexual exploits of his most cherished object (the white woman) to pacify the Black players. If the nineteenth century Ku Klux Klan could see what is happening they would explode in anger. After all, many of the lynchings that took place throughout the south were done because it was believed some Black man had soiled the purity of the white woman. In 1955, the two butchers that murdered 15year old Emmitt Till in Money,

Mississippi, admitted in an interview with *Look* magazine
after they were acquitted, they did it to protect the purity
of the white woman. Till had told them that he had a white
girlfriend back in Chicago. The poor innocent boy even
showed them a picture of her. The two savages confessed
that their intention was not to kill Till for whistling at one of
their wives, but only to scare him. But after he told them of
his youthful escapades with the young white girl, they
shouted to him that he would not live to see the break of
day, and he didn't.

If one observes the immature behavior of Black
players in Canada, one would practically believe that Black
men are obsessed with an uncontrollable attraction to
white women. And the women display the same behavior.
With many women it is like a delicious curiosity. They have
to experience sex with the big, Black, athlete, whose skills
far surpass any they have witnessed in their white
counterpart. I have watched as Black players abandon their
Black wife and family back in the states and stay in Canada
with their newly discovered love, if you dare call it that.

Oftentimes, the women will become nurse maids to
the players. If they get cut from the team and no other
team will pick them up they become a burden on the
women. Many of them lack other skills. Black players for
the most part are not like their white counterparts who
leave the league and then walk into another career because
they have prepared themselves for that day when they no
longer can play ball. Black players often have to agree to
seek no other work outside football in order to get a visa to
play in Canada. They adopt a life of leisure, playing internet
games and slowly wasting away while naïve white women

take care of them. Sometimes white women will use the players as a means to get green cards to come to the United States. So the relationship is reciprocal, often benefitting the woman and sometimes the player. In the long run, however, the player often comes out on the losing side of these relationships. My fellow team mate and friend, Ray Jacobs, is a perfect example.

Ray and I played together for the Calgary Stampede. He wasn't married, but had a girlfriend in North Carolina. Even though his girlfriend was Black, he would often admit that he had an affinity for white women. The coaches knew that and played on his weakness. He dated numerous white women at the same time. Three of them became pregnant and made him a father three times over, in addition to his family in North Carolina. When his playing days were over, Ray returned to the states. The three women decided to collaborate, and just as if they were a team, took him into Canadian courts and got a judgment for back child support payments. He owed over $100,000.00. As of this writing, the North Carolina courts are cooperating with Canada in their attempts to collect the support. Ray has no means to pay this money so he is being threatened with jail time, as if that will help him make payments. Those of us close to Ray wonder how a foreign country can demand child support payments in the United States and the North Carolina courts recognize their claim. We think we know the answer. It is bad enough to the white man that Ray was bedding three of his women it is even worse that they had children by him and now can not collect support from him. If Ray has to go to jail it is a travesty of our justice system.

For many Black players, the CFL is their last or only

hope for fame, money, and glory. If they can't find some semblance of success in Canada, they have to put the cleats up and try to find something else to do. This is a very difficult pill to swallow when your entire life has been wrapped around a game, a simple game, where eleven men line up across from each other and try to take an oblong ball 100 yards to glory. I must admit that at times I got caught up in the lights and the glory of the game. While in Canada my goal was always to return to the states and play again in the NFL. But after awhile there was a different fire burning deep inside of me and that was to write about all the garbage the Black man has to endure in order to maintain a life under the lights. The same garbage you endure in the National Football League you also encounter in Canada. It doesn't change, just the faces and the uniforms. After a while the CFL becomes your way of slapping the NFL in the face. You want to do great things so that your coaches back home will know they made a mistake. You may be underpaid and beat up, but you have gone beyond the motivation of money and fame because until a football player wins the respect of his peers, he has no respect as a player at all. As you play countless years in the CFL, friends and associates begin to ask "why don't you retire?" But you feel the need to leave a legacy. It is not a matter of breaking records or making money in a league where there is none, but when the lights go out and the seats are empty, you want your name to always echo within that arena.

Chapter Four

**SLAVERY AND CHRISTIAN PLAYERS IN THE NATIONAL
FOOTBALL LEAGUE**

*"For all the suffering that Africa and her
descendants endured throughout the centuries, from
slavery, imperialism, colonization, to the Berlin Conference, I
am happy to announce that they are all going to Heaven
first class."—AP*

One of the most potent weapons used by the
oppressors against Black Africans caught in the terrible vice
of slavery was Christianity. Notice that I use the designation
of Christianity and not religions or spirituality, because it
was perceived Christians, followers of Jesus Christ, who
terrorized a nation of people through invasion of their
country and imprisonment of its people. Christianity has
been used as the justification to invade countries, slaughter
its inhabitants, rape their women, and essentially steal their
land. The great crusades were carried out in the name of
Christianity, all of South America was invaded in the name
of Christianity, and the entire Native American population
was practically wiped out, and those that survived were
forced to live on reservations, in the name of Christianity.

Slaves were taught to obey their masters based on the teachings in the New Testament of the Bible. Christianity is a very potent drug that makes the oppressed feel good about their oppression and teaches them to love their oppressor. During the famous civil rights movement of the 1960's, Black folks would gather in a church, sing spirituals and gospel hymns, then listen to a preacher tell them to have courage when they marched out of the church, into the streets and took the devil on with his dogs, guns, and nightsticks. It really wasn't the passivity and non-violent marches that finally got the government to pass civil rights legislation. I would argue it was the fear of violence perpetrated by the Nation of Islam and Malcolm X. When white America looked at Malcolm X and considered his belligerent tone as opposed to Dr. King, they chose to compromise with the latter and give him what he wanted. Without Malcolm X there never could have been a successful King. The United States is not a country that really respects the passive and peaceful nature of people, it instead responds much better to violence. If Black slaves had not fought back during slavery by burning down the cotton fields and causing havoc to the economy of the south, those capitalists would have never realized it was in their economic interest to free the slaves and offer them some kind of salary. That is exactly what happened after the civil war in the form of sharecropping. Christianity has inhibited Black Americans more than it has helped them. It is one of the more effective tools used by coaches of professional football teams to keep the players in check. The National Football League is now over 65% Black and the last thing owners want to happen is to have those players

SLAVERY AND CHRISTIAN PLAYERS IN THE NATIONAL
FOOTBALL LEAGUE

rebel against the plantation conditions on those teams.

I once considered myself a Christian football player and during the first part of my career I stayed passive to the conditions I encountered in the NFL. After seven years in the NFL I finally found myself having to migrate north to the CFL, where for years I continued to explore my spiritual gifts and personal accountability as opposed to being fixated on an event that happened thousands of years ago. In my final years with Calgary I began to come into my own. I woke up from a religious dungeon and discovered the God within me. I began to understand what happens to the Black players and how we succumb to our passivity, refusing to question and fight back. At that point I began to grow spiritually and intellectually. I became a self-made man, with natural knowledge relying more on my spirituality and the God within me, than Jesus outside of my essence. As I begin to talk privately with other players on this subject it became very clear that many of the ball players share this same manner of thinking, preferring to be treated as individuals and not robots. With the recent revelations by the late and great Reggie White, more Black players will begin to move away from the Christianity forced on them from childhood right up to the present time. For years Reggie was the poster player for organizations like Athletes for Christianity. However, after Reggie hung up the helmet and the cleats his outlook began to change. He moved away from the "faith in sports" movement he helped to advance during his years in the league. Reggie felt that he had been "Prostituted" for many years by evangelical groups and sports ministries, all in the name of Jesus Christ. I now wonder why, if we still have a living Jesus, he didn't come down from Heaven and put a stop to this merciless exploitation of Black athletes. Evangelical football players like Reggie before his transformation and others are no threat to the system. Neither are the thousands of Black ministers who call their flock to church on Sunday, sing, dance, flail away praising Jesus, and they leave out two hours later no better off than when they entered the church. The reason is that white America does not fear what it controls. White Americans view the followers of Christ as passive souls with their eyes fixed on Jesus, very peaceful people, content with the status quo. Like the ministers and the flock, Black Christian players fit into that category. They are non-threatening and passive, refusing to believe their plight is one of a slave on the plantation or a professional football field.

I used to see players carrying Bibles under their arms daily in the locker room, but in reality 95% were hypocrites. Understand athletes don't carry Bibles because of their intense commitment to Christianity. They carry them in order to impress the coaches. It's a tool used to protect their position on the team and give a false since of high morality; this goes for both white and black players. To the coaches the Bible toting player is not a threat to his regime of order and tyrannical control. In any locker room on any given day in the NFL or the CFL you can observe Black players with Bibles under their arms. It is simply a case of sustainability. Two equally talented players vying for the same position are forced to use other methods to win out over the other. The Bible is one of those methods. When I begin expressing my personal philosophy during practice and having deep discussions at Bible study sessions,

none of the other players would join me. But after the
debates were over, many of them would approach me and
say "You were right AP. That man was talking nothing but a
bunch of bull shit." They, like I used to be, are still living in
that religious dungeon labeled as a religious conformist.
Being dishonest to themselves doesn't outweigh the need
for a huge paycheck, the roar of the crowd, and the never
ending number of women (especially white women)
available to them.

I must admit many of my teammates sincerely
believed what they heard in those sessions and when they
carried their Bibles, it was not a sham. These are the
players for which I have the greatest amount of compassion
because they are truly the lost ones. These are the players
who believe they are nothing without Jesus. They mirror
the slaves and generations of Blacks after slavery who also
believed they were nothing without Jesus. These are the
Blacks who put down their racial identity because they are
really ashamed to be Black. They dislike their skin color and
the texture of their hair because they believe being white
with straight hair is prettier and superior to Black and
coarse hair. It would be laughable if it wasn't so tragic that
Black people are the only oppressed people in the world
who want to look more like their oppressor than
themselves. They can't change their skin color or the
texture of their hair (even though some try with all kinds of
chemicals) but they can identify with their oppressor by
believing in his Jesus. I wonder how many Black churches
still have a picture of a white Jesus hanging in the sanctuary
in front of all the members, so whenever they look up at the
minister or the choir, they will also see a white Jesus. The

liberation theology movement tried to change that by placing images of a Black Jesus in their churches. Most Christians looked on in amazement and consternation. After all, there is no way Jesus could have been a dark skinned man with coarse hair. That would not fit in with the images of love, peace and beauty perpetrated by Corporate America.

Christian ballplayers must ask themselves what Jesus has truly saved them from and make a list. When I see Christian ball players, I see borderline mental illness because they constantly recite to themselves, "I am nothing without Jesus; all my hopes are in Jesus, all my future doings are in Jesus." They actually place their aspirations in the past and wonder why the spirit has not yet answered their prayers and brought their desires into fruition. Where is the trust and strength in them? It is buried under religious dogma.

Spirituality can inspire a man to take action outside of religious control and denomination to gather all in agreement, and take his case to Washington, D.C., knock on the White House door and demand reparations for those that believe in this debate. They should stay there at the doorstep of the most powerful office in the world and demand their ancestors' wages, the slave labor that made the United States the richest nation in the world. Dr. Martin Luther King, Jr., put it best in his 1963 speech at the Lincoln Memorial. He talked of the un-cashed check America has given Black folks for over a hundred years. He articulated the number of times that Blacks have been promised equality based on their commitment to fight for democracy and once the battle was over they went to cash in and were told there were insufficient funds. It is because of the bad check that our ghettoes are overflowing with Black men and women. The prison system is inundated with our young, and the high school drop out rate and teenage pregnancy run rampant. When the Christian followers join the others in this endeavor, then that will be the kind of Jesus we need. Remember that Jesus had a movement, but there is no movement today. Imagine the repercussions if all Black Christian players in sports began talking about reparations. They would probably get kicked out of the league or something would get done. I don't believe American sports fans would tolerate sports without the Black athlete. And if they would, the games would be dull and boring. But there is no need to worry because the owners have their ammunition in the Black athletes' desire for fame, money, women and their Jesus.

I once gave a Bible study class and it turned out to be a deep discussion on religion, philosophy, America, and Jesus. Deep down inside I wanted the talks to go in this direction because it allowed every player to express his personal philosophy without feeling afraid of being judged. Malcolm X said he wished he had awakened his people before trying to organize them. How can you lead and direct people who are in the dark? On another occasion I got into a heated debate with another player who was a dedicated follower of Jesus.

"When did Christianity begin?" I asked him.

He looked me right in the eyes as if he were going to strike me. He scowled at me, "Christianity started the day my Lord and Savior Jesus Christ died."

I returned his glare and retorted, "Have you read or

studied anything other than the Bible?"

His response was, "That's a sin. You're doing the devil's work when you question the accuracy of the Bible and the love Jesus has for us." He paused as we continued our stare down of each other. "A.P. [that's what the players called me] Jesus is all I have and I'm not going to question nothing or read nothing else to take me away from my God, the Lord Jesus."

He was so sincere and passive I asked him, "Where is the God in You?"

He answered, "It is in Jesus."

"Where's Jesus?" I continued my questioning.

"Jesus is God," he answered emphatically as if having delivered the last word on the subject.

I put on my helmet and walked away because the coach called my name for a drill. We were in the middle of practice. Later that evening after practice, I reflected back on our conversation. I felt sorry for my teammate, putting all his future and strength in a man that some say never existed, thus making his own future and strength something that will never have power because the source you communicate with and command must deliver every time.

On another occasion, also in Canada, some other players accepted what I was expressing at that time. They agreed that I did give them something to think about, which was often a foreign concept to men who only concentrated on hitting another person instead of engaging in debate with them. I told them that the Bible instructs us to seek and ye shall find, meaning you can find your own truth in time. I told them that I wish I had sought knowledge on my own before because my life would have been much easier to control on my own terms. We all have been misled regarding the true history of Christianity. It did not start with the crucifixion of Jesus Christ. He was not crucified on a cross, but hung from a tree, in the same manner in which Blacks have been hung from trees. Christianity began in Rome in 325 A.D. where men sat down and decided what people should believe in. Out of the meetings came the compromised Nicene Creed. All bishops with the exception of two decided that Jesus was not a "creature" as other human beings, but was the son of God created through divine intervention. This description of Jesus as God's son is later articulated in the Apostle's Creed, "I believe in God, the Father almighty. I believe in Jesus Christ, His only son." This creed makes it impossible for human beings to attain a one on one relationship with God. We can only do that through Jesus Christ his son. Blacks and whites share in this Christian interpretation, which is merely a compromise between contending forces in 325 A.D. It is still taught in our churches today, and is believed by Blacks throughout this country. The Nicene Creed started much of the evangelical Christian movement throughout the world. The supporters of this movement called themselves crusaders. They were standing on the foundation of Christianity, they were riding the back of Jesus, they took the cross, turned it upside down, sharpened it into a sword, and went out spreading the Gospel while that same sword was dripping blood, and it still is.

I further told my teammates that one of the great thinkers of the Twentieth Century, Dr. W.E.B. DuBois, also questioned the legitimacy of Christianity as a basis for Black American's salvation and freedom. Christianity is the spiritual component of capitalism, an economic system that personifies suffering of Black people globally. It was Christian European nations that met in Berlin in 1885 and divided Africa among themselves, just as if the continent was not already occupied. Dr. DuBois advanced the general thesis that linked the continued political and economic exploitation of Africa with the expansion of European imperialism and war. Throughout his illustrative life, Dr. DuBois recognized the futility in accepting both Christianity and capitalism as the path to Black economic equality in the United States.

After my talks some players walked away saying, "A.P's going to get us cut," meaning we're going to lose our jobs listening to that "nigga." But others said, "A.P. keep on going with this. I'm feeling you brotha." One brother's eyes watered because words I spoke were the truth, and truth often will make people cry.

Late at night and after practice when I was alone with just my thoughts, the real me would take control and take my mind to the land of truth. I'd close my eyes and visualize the Asians in Asia. They were at peace. Then I saw the Native Americans, both north and south. There were great civilizations—the Incas, the Mayas, the Aztecs, and the Eskimos—and they also were at peace. I then traveled across the ocean and saw my people, the Africans, living on their continent in tranquility. Then I viewed the whites in Europe and unlike the other people, they were restless. Inhabitants of the world were in their way and they had to take what others possessed. Using their advanced technology of death and destruction, they began to conquer other people. The loud explosion from their weapons awakened the Asians. They killed the Native Americans and captured the Africans forcing them into a state of slavery. And in Asia, the Americas, and on the African continent it was written in the soil, *Revelations 6:2, "I looked and behold a white horse. He who sat on it had a bow and a crown was given to him and he went out conquering and to conquer."* I saw the crusaders and their movement conquering everything in their path, and in the Caucasus Mountains I saw *Revelation 6:4, "Another horse fiery red went out. And it was granted to the one who sat on it to take peace from the earth and that people should kill one another, and there was given to him a great sword."* The white warrior went all through Asia and sailed to America, north and south, to conquer those lands. After his conquest, he looked toward Africa and saw riches in the land and the people. He invaded the African continent, destroyed the civilization and depleted the country of its most healthy and physical warriors. They were barbarians terrorizing a civilized people, and now they talk of their advanced civilization. The Africans were put on ships and the man that piloted the ship was named John Hawkins. His boat was named Jesus. When the slaves arrived in the new world they began to sing that great hymn, "Steal Away to Jesus." They were not talking about a man, but the ship Jesus to take them back home. Spirituals were based on the desire of the Africans to return to their home land. Now we have gospels that express the Blacks desire to escape the oppression of a capitalistic state. That is why other people laugh at Blacks who get caught up "with the holy ghost" in church. Scenes in movies depicting Blacks at worship show them shouting, dancing, turning flips, and shaking their bodies until they literally fall out. They are trying to wake up Jesus and bring Him back. We have caught the white man's religion, Christianity, and now beg to a man who died hanging from a tree, to save us. Instead of rebelling against our oppressor we have joined him through our acceptance of his culture, to include his religion. We have totally jettisoned our cultural heritage from Africa and become the darker version of the ugly American. One of the tragedies of the Iraq and the Vietnam Wars was that Black men went into those countries and killed other men of color who had done nothing to them. And these men did it for a system that has oppressed and kept them down for centuries. We must take seriously the meaning found in *Revelations 6:8, "So I looked and behold a pale horse and the name of him who sat on it was death, and hell followed with him and power was given to them over a fourth of the earth to kill with the sword, with hunger, with death, and by the beasts of the earth."*

The rulers of this country are now trying to get to the moon, Mars, and other solar systems. If they succeed, they will destroy those entities just as they are slowly destroying the planet earth. Technology and greed is the Achilles heel of America. These very people have the power to destroy all of us with their arsenal of nuclear weapons. When a nuclear bomb goes into the atmosphere, it carries a certain number of nuclear war heads and each war head has a designated target to destroy. It goes up like a rocket and falls like stars. When the rulers of this world feel power and control is no longer within their grasp, this world will end. This gives meaning *to Revelation 6:13,14, "And the stars of Heaven fell to the earth as a fig tree drops its late*

SLAVERY AND CHRISTIAN PLAYERS IN THE NATIONAL
FOOTBALL LEAGUE

figs when it is shaken by a mighty wind; then the sky receded as a scroll when it is rolled up and every mountain and island was moved out of its place."

Black Christian football players perceive themselves as crusaders. I once found myself in that same arena convincing men to put their faith in a religion instead of having faith in themselves. Instead of Bible study after practice the Black athlete needs to study the history of himself so he can look up and understand how he got in this place, and where he stands today. Knowledge is power. History reflects the future. Truth gives revelations. Without those two ingredients, we fail as a whole.

I find it rather ironical that these Black football players and others who claim to be followers of Christ wear ear rings and tattoos all over their body. In the Old Testament piecing the ear of a slave meant you owned that slave for life. When I watch Black athletes being interviewed on national television wearing diamond ear rings, I am reminded of the Black work horse that is physically strong but mentally weak. The law concerning slaves in the Old Testament was expressed in Exodus 21: 5-6 as follows: "But if the slave plainly says 'I love my master, my wife, and my children, I will not go free,' then his master shall bring him to the judges. He shall also bring him to the door, or to the doorpost, and the master shall pierce his ear with an awl: and he shall serve him forever."

I may be the only Christian that notices on NFL Sunday when a Christian athlete scores a touchdown, and points to the Heavens, thanking God for a divine advantage, yet he is wrapped in secular tattoos glorifying things Christ would oppose. Jesus did not have a tattoo, nor did He pierce his ears. Jesus was a master of his own destiny, tapping into the divine power given to Him by God. Athletes and many other inner city folks will never reach that divine power that lies dormant within them when they create superficial symbols to build up a weakened identity. They will remain in a spiritual ghetto no matter how much money or how much fame they achieve when they wear their insecurities and suffering right on their body. In Leviticus 19-28, God instructs man not to "cut your bodies for the dead or put tattoo marks on yourselves. I am the Lord."

Chapter Five

MICHAEL VICK AND THE PRISON FOOTBALL LEAGUE

"I believe every man should judge himself, because a man was never empowered to judge others, however, if you're inspired to give opinion, entertain them with facts." —
AP

Why do so many Black athletes, from Jack Johnson at the turn of the Twentieth Century to Michael Vick today, have less than happy endings to their careers? We Black professionals begin on a high optimistic note, energized and dedicated to do the best we can, but too often our dreams end up as nightmares. The predominantly white fans in this country love the white athlete but only tolerate the Black one and that toleration is based on those players conforming to certain standards established by the ruling class. Michael Vick was probably the finest all around athlete to ever play in the NFL. Vick is now in jail, typical of the tragic endings for many of our heroes. Jack Johnson goes to prison, Joe Louis is dogged by the IRS even after serving as an exemplary soldier during World War II, Darryl Strawberry becomes a victim of the crack epidemic, Bob Hayes, one of the greatest wide receivers goes to prison and famed coach Tom Landry refuses to assist him, Barry Bonds is being plagued with charges of steroid use, and now Vick is in prison for sponsoring dog fights in Virginia. Why do so many Black athletes find themselves in trouble with the law and in poverty after lucrative careers? This kind of behavior is symptomatic of individuals caught in the pathological lifestyle found in inner city communities. One might then surmise that athletes return to the environment in which they were raised or then again, they may never leave despite a very lucrative career in sports. This is true even when they move out of the inner city and into mansions; they carry that pathological behavior with them.

There is an old adage that the "apple doesn't fall far from the tree." When Marcus Vick got into trouble at Virginia Tech the world wondered about his older brother Michael. For a while I thought maybe the older brother would escape that same kind of pathological behavior since he had made it into the NFL and was walking around with a 137 million dollar contract. I thought maybe the tree grew on a hill, and when Marcus fell from the tree he just rolled down with the rest of the spoiled apples, and Michael was fortunate enough to stay atop where the good men remain. But maybe that was wishful thinking on my part. I so wanted to see this polished athlete develop to his fullest and become one of the NFL's greatest quarterbacks ever. But somehow the rotten apples had rubbed off on him and just like Jack and Jill, he came tumbling down the hill. It makes you search for answers to a troubling problem and, that is, how damaged are these men in their earlier years before hitting the big leagues and all the fame and money, but still cannot escape their past. If we can find the answer then we might be able to begin to deal with the destructive nihilistic behavior that so many of our young Black men possess. It is this behavior that leads them to the prison, drugs, or death, no matter what their station in life: drug dealer, crack addict, or professional athlete.

Michael Vick represents what the majority of young Americans' dream of achieving; that is money, fame, and stardom. For young Black men he is the role model for success, not for his contributions to community, because of that very large 137 million dollar contract he signed. Especially the young men from the "hood" can admire him just like they admire the successful pimp or drug dealer. They all represent the same things, money, women, and bling. Vick is the poster child for what happens when you give a young Black man from the streets of Newport News, Virginia, or any central city for that matter, that much money and all the freedom that goes with it. Instead of escaping that pathological influence of the streets, Vick brought it with him. He didn't seem to understand that you cannot sign a contact for millions of dollars and continue to smoke weed. And Vick is not the only Brother caught up in this web. Lawrence Phillips, a great running back out of Nebraska with a promising career, is now in prison, Michael Irving did jail time for smoking crack cocaine, Nate Newton is in prison on conviction of distribution of marijuana, Charles Jordan, who played with me in Oakland, was in prison for attempted murder; and Alan Iverson came right out of prison and went to Georgetown and is now one of the greatest NBA players in the history of the game.

In 2008, the parade of potential players for the Prison Football League continues. Plaxico Burress, The New

York Giant wide receiver, who caught the winning touchdown in the 2007 Super Bowl game, may well serve a mandatory three years in a New York prison for carrying an unlicensed weapon into a New York City night club. The Prison Football League now has three of its skilled position players behind bars, Michael Vick at quarterback, Lawrence Phillips at running back, and soon to be Plexico Burress as the wide receiver. The prison's problem will be filling all the offensive line positions because they are usually composed of white players. For some reason they escape the crime and vice involved with organized sports. No doubt they do their share of unlawful acts, but never seem to get caught or make the news. I am not suggesting a conspiracy exists against Black players. There would be no reason for the Giants to want Burress in prison, nor the Falcons to want Vick behind bars. After all, they are the super stars of their teams and help make them winners. It is the forces outside the National Football League that have these players under surveillance.

No one player has been under white America's microscope than O. J. Simpson and they finally got him. The Simpson sentence has to be one of the worst miscarriages of justice in American legal history. We all know O.J. was not given 9 to 30 years for robbing other crooks for sports memorabilia that may have belonged to him. O.J. was given those years because white America feels they were denied the right to put him behind bars 13 years ago because of a Black jury that, according to the self-proclaimed protectors of a justice system that has no problem throwing Black men in jail, but frowns on doing the same to their own, failed to put him away. A right wing columnist Cal Thomas blatantly said as much in an article he wrote. Commenting on District Judge Jackie Glass' statement that the sentence had nothing to do with his previous, Thomas wrote "maybe not in her eyes, but in the eyes of virtually everyone else who believes the earlier verdict as a miscarriage of justice, this trial was just deserts." His statement is stunning to any one who believes that our constitution guards against double jeopardy. One has to admit that O.J. wasn't the smartest person around. But his biggest error was failure to realize that America has a dual system of justice, one for whites and another for Blacks and it seems especially for Black athletes. The pathetic aspect to Thomas' statement is that he feels there is something self-righteous in his assertion that justice can be served after this system said the man was innocent. With Simpson gone, now the American people will be watching Plaxico Burress and Barry Bonds go to trial. The Prison Football system gets closer to reality with each trial and conviction. Not only the Prison Football system, but Bonds makes it possible to begin looking at baseball also.

There has always been a discrepancy in the law as it applies to Blacks and whites. Congressman John Conyers of Detroit has been persistent in his attempts to even the punishment for using powder and crack cocaine. Sentencing for the latter has been more severe because it is recognized as a Black drug, where as powder cocaine is the preferred drug of the whites in the suburbs. Recently, in a small town in Texas a young white girl was placed on probation after burning down her parent's home, while a young Black girl was originally given 20 years for fighting a white hall monitor at the local high school. The Black community was so irate, they ultimately changed that decision. With such discrepancies in our larger society, why wouldn't we find the same within the sports world. Black ball players must learn to be more cautious in their behavior off the field.

A majority of these players come out of the same kind of stereotypical environment, Section 8(a) housing, crime, drugs, drive-by shooting and overwhelming influence of gangs. Even though Vick was able to escape that influence because of his early athletic ability and a concerned father and mother, some of the negative environment seeped into his system, so that when he did make it in the pro's he couldn't break that kind of influence on him. When you witness men with tremendous talent and great careers who succumb to the evils that lurk at all times in the inner cities, you realize just how powerful the negative influences are with our young. If someone with the ability and opportunity of Vick fall prey to the slime crawling around in his environment, what are the chances that a young man who can not read or write and has no physical talents can escape? Many of our young men are caught in the trap of having muscles with no mind, a brain with no brilliance, and a spirit without spirituality. They are lost and do not know how to find themselves. As a result, breaking laws and ignoring the rules of an orderly society and going to prison become a rite of passage in our communities. "You did time and now you're the man" is the creed among our young. Iconic figures such as Vick don't help the situation when they do silly things like conduct dog fights right in the face of the authorities. Vick should have been hanging out with men and women who could help him leverage that salary into wealth instead of using it on activities inimical to his future success. He ends up having to declare bankruptcy after having access to over one hundred and thirty million dollars. That is shameful behavior and it happens all too often with our athletes.

Since the incident with the dogs, Vick has stated publicly that he needed to grow up. I agree and respect the man for his honesty. At least he didn't try to blame others for his actions. We all have those moments in our lives for which we are ashamed and wish we could reverse them. As Black people caught in this trap for centuries, we are always trying to find a reason for what others view as our pathological behavior. Some could argue what is the big thing with dog fights when this country once sanctioned "coon hunts." During slavery, plantation owners would participate in a sport called "coon hunting." In this sport the Black man's speed was pitted against the white man's perceived superior knowledge and exceptional use of weapons. The sport was also used as a way to make sure that the slaves always obeyed. A recalcitrant slave would be subjected to the game while the other slaves watched on in fear. A slave with whom a owner was dissatisfied would be swabbed down with a specific scent. He would be given a few hours to run at night, then the owners would gather with their hound dogs and begin the search. Bets would be placed on whose hound dog could find the runaway first. If hiding up a tree, once found, the man would be shot down like any other animal. Against the backdrop of that history, Vick's crime seems minor. The difference is that the white folks wrote the laws, and once the magnitude of "coon hunting" was exposed, it was stopped. But no one was ever punished for the crime. During the first few decades of the Twentieth Century, in Rosewood, Florida, a wild game of "coon hunting" lasted for as long as eight days, with more than 100 Blacks being killed.(Claude Anderson, *Black Wealth, White Labor*, August 1994, pg., 216: PowerNomics Corporation of America, Bethesda, Maryland). Ultimately, the Florida State Legislature provided reparations for the families of the victims, but no one was ever punished or ostracized as some kind of demonic person as has happened with Vick.

When Vick went before the judge, he was coached by others to be humble and contrite. When he pleaded guilty, the judge quickly reminded him that with a guilty plea he'd have to live with whatever sentence was handed him. The problem is that we have been living with what they have given us for over 400 years, and they always fail to recognize what we have given this country. I am not trying to defend Michael Vick's actions, but I believe he should have told that judge, "Yes judge I am guilty from a psychological perspective, from a slave's perspective, and from a survivor of Jim Crow's perspective. I'm guilty of trying to be like you. I couldn't do unto the "massa" what he has done unto me, my children, my mothers, my fathers, and my grandparents. Oh yes, I am guilty of emulating you, the "massa."

"I was hanging dogs, the same way the "massa" was hanging me!

I was shooting dogs, the same way the "massa" was shooting me!

I was drowning dogs, the same way the "massa" drowned me in the Mississippi River!

77

MICHAEL VICK AND THE PRISON FOOTBALL LEAGUE

I buried dogs, the same way the "massa" buried me in unmarked graves!

I allowed dogs to lie in their own blood; the same way the "massa" allowed me to lie in my own blood!

The chances are good that Michael Vick will be eligible for parole in the spring of 2009. The question, however, remains will any General Manager want to take the risk of signing him to a contract? And even if he is willing to take the risk will the owners welcome him back? Their dilemma is a quandary over profits as opposed to public acceptance. Vick will be 29 when he is eligible for release from prison, so there is a good possibility that his talents will still be intact. In fact he will undoubtedly play prison football and stay in good shape. The problem is that white America is tired of seeing Black criminals making millions of dollars, bragging about how great they are, living next door to them, and watching their daughters have mixed babies. They would rather see Blacks perform from a safer distance such as inside the prison. They would prefer to let the athlete out on Sunday for their entertainment and then returned to their jail cell, their cage, their dungeon, a safe distance from them and their vulnerable daughters.

Michael Vick represents a new paradigm that could be fully developed by the year 2030. What is taking so long to implement this plan? They need a sufficient amount of young and vibrant super studs to perform their exceptional athletic abilities from behind bars. They still get the glory and the fame, but not the freedom to lurk among the civilized people. Michael Vick may be the man to implement their plan. This paradigm was outlined long before Vick became the first test case. Remember these words in a song, "they're smiling in your face, all the time, they want to take your place, the back stabbers." The architects of Vick's future are smiling because they can begin to implement their plan. By the year 2030, with the rate Blacks are going to prison, there will be approximately 2.3 million Black men in prison. That will be the population used to establish the Prison Football League. It will be similar to the Roman Coliseums with competition between the prisoners as athletes. Gone will be the cocky athlete driving the Lamborghini, bragging about how much money he has, and how many of the "massa's" women he is bedding down. So many young children are going to desire to be a part of the PFL they will deliberately commit crimes just to be a part of the league and play alongside of one of the greats at that time. The outside world will continue to sell merchandise, i.e., jersey's (Michael Vick jerseys are still being sold while he is in prison). There will be PFL trading cards and play stations. The owners and wardens will not have to share the profits with the players, because, just like during slavery, the performers have nothing coming to them for their labor. The plantation system is already at work in the prisons of America. The prototype is the Federal Prison Factory system under the auspices of a corporation called UNICOR. Under this system, federal inmates work for the factory producing goods to be sold to federal agencies. UNICOR produces uniforms for the military, trucks for border patrol, and generators for the United States Air Force. These products represent only a small fraction of what UNICOR produces behind bars. The inmates who work for UNICOR receive 23 cents an hour. This is much like the convict/lease program that existed throughout the south after the Civil War into the 20th Century. This is slave labor. It can be duplicated in professional sports. The talent pool is deep, and inmates would jump at the opportunity to perform on national television creating a feeling of performing just like they have already dreamed of doing. Talented men like Vick will be the nucleus of the Prison Football League.

The righteous man may fall seven times but will always rise again. Since Vick failed seven seasons in the NFL to win a Super Bowl Championship as a free man, maybe if he is rebuilt behind bars, he can repair the self-inflicted damages by rising in the Prison Football League. Vick is being rebuilt in the image of the master controlled slaves on the plantation. Prison life in America for Black men is a modern day plantation. There may be a new platform, a new stage, and a new era for Michael Vick. His career is not over, but may be just beginning. He is at the door step of becoming one of the modern day wonders of the world, an athlete you cannot touch or get an autograph from, because he is too far away. He is in the prison where he can do no further damage and is no longer a threat to the white world that wants to see him perform on the field but does not want him loose within the society. He lives within his ruined career, his faults, his conviction, and his lack of awareness. It may serve as some consolation to Vick knowing that he will soon be able to perfect his game by throwing a few out routes to Plexico Burress. I end with *Amos 9 verse 11, "On that day I will raise up the tabernacle of David, which has fallen down, and repair its damages; I will raise up its ruins, and rebuild it as in the days of old.*

Chapter Six

THE PURCHASE (FORT JESUS)

"To conquer a man is to give him a future not of his choosing." AP

I would like to believe that at one point in time, right on this planet, people loved each other. When a child was born God granted him/her the earth and all the fullness within. The concept of greed, hoarding and claiming ownerships were not in God's divine plans. Everything He made was for the entire race of people. The water, the vegetables, the fruit, and the land were given to us by the Heavenly Father. Why then have we placed a price tag on nature's abundance when God favors no one group over the other? He doesn't have social classes or economic classes. That is a man made concept. To trade in human flesh is an abomination against God and is detrimental to His purpose for all living beings on earth.

It is strange to me that, here in the United States, the white population wants to act like slavery never existed. When the subject comes up they will always respond in the same manner, "I never owned slaves, my ancestors never owned slaves, so why bring it up with me." In fact, to hear whites talk about slavery is like listening to a repeat of the same phrase, "my ancestors didn't get to this country until the Twentieth Century," or "my ancestors were dirt farmers during slavery and struggled just like the slaves." What a real joke that is, free men struggling like slaves. To enslave another human being is the lowest level to which a person can stoop and the white population stooped that low for over 250 years in America. In all fairness, I guess if I were white and was the owner of such an ugly past, I would want to deny its existence also. Recently the United States House of Representatives passed a resolution apologizing for slavery and many conservatives responded by claiming that was a waste of time. They should have been concentrating on the war, gas prices, and every other problem confronting this county. The bottom line, however, is that the residuals of slavery still exist in crime, poor education, and dilapidated living conditions for the children of the slaves. Black and white conservatives alike now argue that the plight of Black America lies in its own hands and if there is poverty and crime it is its own fault. Nothing can be further from the truth. The overwhelming problems are a direct result of the 250 years of slavery and another one hundred years of the most sickening form of apartheid only surpassed by that which existed in South Africa. Dr. DuBois challenged these "blame the victim" assertions as early as 1910 when he wrote, "For three centuries this people (whites) lynched Blacks who dared to be brave, raped Black women who dared to be virtuous, crushed dark skinned youth who dared to be ambitious, and encouraged and made flourish servility, lewdness, and apathy" (DuBois, *Conservation of the Races*). DuBois further argued that if society could rid itself of racism which to him was the socioeconomic roots of moral degeneracy, then Blacks would thrive in proportion to the success ratios of every other ethnic group in America. That, of course, has not happened.

Contrary to the desires of white America the pathologies that exist within the African American communities can be traced back to Jesus. It was at Fort Jesus that the miserable suffering and loss of freedom started for proud Black people in Africa. Fort Jesus was built by the Portuguese in 1499 and its sole purpose was to house African slaves before they shipped out in the holes of Slave ships for the west. It is located in East Kenya on Mombassa Island. From an air view, Fort Jesus was constructed in the shape of a man. Inside is like a dungeon where the captured slaves we held against their will. Fort Jesus was designed by an Italian named Jao Batisto. It was his final project for the Portuguese Army. Batisto was clever in his design. The cells where the slaves we jailed, had only one way out. They became known as the "tunnels of no return." The slaves would always try to escape so Batisto had tunnels, which the Africans believed to be escape routes, however, these routes would lead them onto ships waiting in the harbor. There is still a bell right in the center of town. It was used to inform the locals to run and hide because the slave catchers were pulling up in a slave ship. The liar, the thief, the murderer was approaching fast. The frightened African was no match against the lethal weapons that the European brought ashore. Once the hunter arrived there was no escape for the hunted.

Jao Batisto named it Jesus for a religious reference. Fort Jesus was his crown jewel, his trademark. Jao was praised for his masterpiece. When honored and praised for his creation, he would always say, "don't thank me, thank Jesus." Today, African Americans throughout the western hemisphere are among the strongest believers in Jesus Christ. Just like Jao suggested his admirers thank Jesus for his deadly creation, so do Blacks thank Jesus for their suffering. There are over 85,000 Black churches that thank the same Jesus, as did Jao, every Sunday. As a child attending church in Riverside, California, I remember hearing the church bells ringing, and listening to the choir from outside march into the church, swaying from side to side, as if they were on a slave ship. There was a time when the bell in the town warned us of impending danger, today we are listening to a different bell, the bell of complacency, the bell of conformity, because somewhere along the way from Africa to America we lost our natural sounds and have settled for an unnatural sound and life. We have become dependent on this same Jesus that Jao gives credit for building his famous dungeon. Professional football players have been so socialized into a world of dependency on Jesus that they call on him during the entire football game. I found the player that would yell and scream the most during the game was more frightened than others and they would constantly recite:

"I will win in the name of Jesus! I will not be injured in the name of Jesus! I will not make a mistake in the name of Jesus! I will give all glory in the name of Jesus! I will make my coach/master proud in the name of Jesus!"

What about the idea of doing things for the sake of just doing them? God has given you free choice to shape your life to your choosing. Football and athletics is not a call to destiny. More than likely Jesus is not going to come back down here and help you win a football game. Where was Jesus during slavery? Why didn't he come back then and eradicate every slave owner and those who supported that institution from the face of the earth. If he didn't get involved in such an insidious practice why in the world would he bother with a football game? The idea that Jesus is not an intercessor in our daily lives does not resonate well with Black athletes because they parallel their activities with the Lord. Just like Jesus was the hope for freedom among the slaves, He now serves as the hope for Black folks often caught in a life of poverty and depravity. Many of the football players come from that background and therefore, depend on Jesus' intervention, when playing a game, in the NFL. Many of these players believe their presence in the sport gives the industry sustainability as Jesus is the sustainer of mankind. On closer examination many of the Black players share many commonalities with Jesus; he was born out of wedlock, he was poor and never knew his father and his mother had children from a different father. Jesus left home at a young age to find himself and ended up becoming a spiritual super star. Many of the sports announcer love to talk about Black players who were born to a single mother, were poor, and never knew their father. They talk of how they leave home at a young age and end up becoming sports super stars.

I call this phenomenon the "Athletic Rapture" where the excelling in athletics by a Black Christian athlete is equivalent to the accession of Jesus Christ, and if you mention the word "slavery" they will laugh at you because in their mind, living in America, with all the wealth and notoriety that comes with playing in the NFL, makes one free from the ills of the free world. These gladiators of the gridiron cling to their Jesus and Christianity as if they will lose all their glory if they lose him. What they fail to recognize is that their status on the football field is comparable to the slave in the cotton field. And whereas they perceive Jesus' assistance as a positive thing, he also offered support to the plantation owners in their justification to the slaves as to why they should accept their lowly status in life. Not once in the New Testament does Jesus condemn slavery as being inimical to the word of God. Jesus actually expresses his approval of slavery. In Matthew 10:24, he states that "A disciple is not above the teacher or a slave his master." And in Matthew 24:45-46, "Who then is the faithful and wise slave, whom his master has put in charge of his household, to give the other slaves their allowance of food at the proper time? Blessed is that slave whom his master will find at work when he arrives."

Following in the footsteps of Jesus, his follower Paul made it even worse for those caught in the grips of slavery by suggesting that the institution of slavery is not only divine, but all slaves should get the idea of freedom out of their minds. In *1 Timothy 6:1-5*, Paul instructs slaves in the following manner: "Let all who are under the yoke of slavery regard their masters as worthy of all honor, so that the name of God and the teaching may not be blasphemed. Those who have believing masters [this I view as an oxymoron] must not be disrespectful to them on the ground that they are members of the church; rather they must serve them all the more, since who benefit by their service are believers and beloved." Again we find in Titus 2:5-10,

"Tell slaves to be submissive to their masters and to give satisfaction in every respect; they are not to talk back, not to pilfer, but to show complete and perfect fidelity, so that in everything they may be an ornament to the doctrine of God our Savior." In the next passage, Paul instructs slaves to obey, no matter how mean and nasty the master may be. "Slaves accept the authority of your masters with all deference not only those who are kind and gentle but also those who are harsh. It is a credit to you if, being aware of God, you endure pain while suffering unjustly.   If you endure when you do right and suffer for it, you have God's approval." I am convinced that this particular scripture was repeated often by the plantation owners. In fact, I wouldn't be surprised if this page was pasted on the door of every slave cabin, so that when the weary got up early in the morning to face a blazing sun and an intemperate slave driver, they would always know that everything would be all right in the next world.

This could also be the words posted in the locker rooms of every professional football team as the players adjust to life on the football plantation. However, I must point out that football players are not the only Blacks who have bought this idea that somehow Jesus will deliver them from the evils of this world.   This belief is pervasive throughout Black America, be it the inner city poverty stricken communities or the bourgeoisie middle class Blacks who now occupy the suburbs of every big city in America. I once attended an upper scale dinner party given by a Black who will remain anonymous. He wanted to show off to his friends by flaunting his association with professional football players. We were the animals on display to the well educated Blacks who Malcolm X constantly criticized. Being aware of their pretensions and Malcolm's warnings I sat at the dinner table and cautiously picked up on their conversation. They loved America, they loved capitalism, and if a Black person couldn't make it in the most wonderful and opportunistic country in the world, then something was wrong with them. I recognized this to be the class that Martin Luther King, Jr., warned us about, the ones who only go to the Black side of town to go to church on Sunday. After dinner we all retired to the quaint and comfortable family room where the conversation turned to just how well we, the Black race, have survived under such awful conditions for the past 400 years in America.

"I believe we have to give all credit to Jesus for being with us all the time during our battles," the hostess said.

"Yes, it is because our ancestors turned to Christianity and rejected all the pagan religions they practiced in Africa that we have survived," another well dressed lady added in a tone of authority.

I began to squirm in the comfortable recliner I had sat in when we retired to the family room. I told myself to remain quiet. After all you are here to be shown off like a trophy and not for your opinion. You are just a football player, someone who performs for the entertainment of the bourgeoisie on Sunday. You are to be seen and not heard.

"Yes, and our churches and ministers did a superb job in taking in our ancestors and making sure they made it through the difficult times after slavery. You know reconstruction was no cake walk," a gray haired elderly man added as he loaded his pipe with tobacco and began to puff

88

on that nauseating instrument.

I had enough of the talk and the smoke. I had to speak out. "Why do you give an invisible entity all the credit for our survival? Maybe our ancestors made it because of their own ingenuity and creativity as well as strength."

The looks on their faces could cut right through me. How dare the instrument of our enjoyment speak out, and actually contradict what we, the educated and elite say. You could see smirks now on their faces and their minds, "We are the Talented Tenth, and you should simply follow our lead."

"You can't be serious?" the same man asked. "Our ancestors made it through those harsh years because they put all their faith in Jesus and were some of the most faithful Christians in this country."

Both his condescending attitude and his arrogance were both annoying. "Was it this same Jesus that sanctioned the suffering on the slave ships, the rapes of our women, and the lynching of our men?" I now asked.

"Shame on you," the old man now scolded me. The other ladies shot him a look as if to say, don't bother, he knows no better, after all he's just an athlete. But the man gave me a disdainful look and his eyebrows furrowed. 'No, the Lord did not prevent those things from happening. But what he did was give our ancestors the strength to endure because they turned to him." He paused for a moment to relight that awful pipe and then continued, "You need only compare our plight to the Native Americans and you see how the Lord rewarded us for our loyalty to him." He paused and looked at all the other guests, probably to make sure he had everyone's attention. After all he was about to

89

become very profound in his deliberations with me. "The Native Americans are not Christians and today they are much worst off than are Blacks. We were Christians and God has rewarded us for our acceptance and service to Jesus the son."

While listening to this man explain why we should be faithful to Christianity my mind wandered to the locker rooms before a game. Football players believe that they will have an advantage over the opponent if they say a prayer and ask for victory in the name of Jesus, just like this old man felt that we had obtained advantage over the Native Americans because we prayed in the name of Jesus. The truth can slap us right in the face, but with generations of conditioning and with deeply entrenched traditions we don't recognize nor are we able to act upon that very truth. Our traditional habits become rooted in our souls and we see nothing else. The traditional truth under the auspices of Christianity has not delivered us from misery and a form of bondage.

I believe that our ancestors survived because of the strength that lay within their souls. In many ways we can say they made it despite Christianity. It seems in many ways Christianity sanctioned their oppression and favored the oppressor. What saved us was the God that is within. I sincerely believe that God dwells in me and in all of us. Our souls, our human bodies are temples that house the most loving and powerful force still being explored and discovered daily. I must protect the God in me, which encourages me to eat, drink, focus upon and pay attention to what my inner spirit tells me is right. When our team would have prayer before a game I did not pray to a Jesus who told my ancestors to endure the evils of slavery and be loyal servants, but to the God within me, who tells me I am every other man's equal, not meant to be his slave. In order to discover the best within me, I could not be a hypocrite and pray for God to let me enjoy victory over someone who undoubtedly He loves as much as He loves me. To hit another man, take his legs right from under him, knowing darn well that he might end up with something broken, or a concussion, is not sanctioned by God, but by the devil. Where the devil dwells, God cannot be found. Wars, crime in the streets, drug houses, football fields, and anyplace where one individual's goal is to do harm to another are the devil's workshops. Many of the readers may question why I place football in the category with such despicable things. I guess it is because the devil is quite clever; somehow he has made it enjoyable to view football players getting injured, and even killed. Fans seek the signatures, the garments, and the equipment of these gladiators, not knowing what they worship is counter to God's teachings. The First Commandment is not to have any false gods before him. Fans have placed these false gods of the gridiron before the Lord and cheer their destruction instead of celebrating God's love. John took Jesus to the Sea of Galilee to be baptized; the coaches take the players to the stadium to be glorified.

The apex of this glorification is the Super Bowl game. At the top of the Super Bowl trophy, better known as the Lombardi Trophy, is a football that points towards the heavens. The winners of that venerable game become part of the select few that are placed in the book of football immortality. It is like the Lambs Book of Life because we

91

become immortalized by the fans of the game, just as Jesus is immortalized in our minds. What the fans, players, coaches, and owners fail to realize is that the glory of the victory and the game will soon fade. Old players must retire and, unless they are chosen for the Hall of Fame, become forgotten. Contemporary fans will not know the teams that played in the second Super Bowl (we always remember the first) let alone the names of many players. After the cheering, the music, and the glory have faded from a player's life he often is left uneducated, impoverished, spiritually broken and uncertain of his future. Just as we finish our athletic careers with success, we have to be victorious outside the arena of sports where the real game of life is played out. I am talking about the mental, intellectual, and spiritual game of life. Football is finite, but what you learn in your life experiences and how you prepare for your spiritual journey is infinite.

There is irony in the name Fort Jesus. What it represents in the Black man's history is a terrible tragedy. That it should be named after the man that those same Blacks came to worship and believe is their salvation is the irony. We experience that same dilemma when we study our history. It was the Christian church that our ancestors turned to for deliverance from slavery. After the United States government reneged on its commitment to provide all slaves with land after the Civil War, land that they rightfully deserved after decades of exploitation, the slaves were left with nothing. Literally, they had no money, no land or food, only a strong spirit and a faith in a person they could not feel, touch, or see. This person, Jesus, was represented through the thousands of churches and preachers who popped up all over the countryside. These preachers told our people to come to church, seek Jesus, and through their faith they will survive. Christians will argue that we have survived, but what is the quality of our lives today? Our communities are racked with pathologies, the schools, the home, and even the church. Drugs are freely sold, prostitution thrives, and gang warfare rules in the inner cities. It is time for Black Americans to examine just how effective the Christian church has been in delivering our people from crime and poverty. Compare Christians to the Nation of Islam and assess which has been more effective. We have a right to do that, not only a right but an obligation.

I believe our communities can be saved but it will take a strong commitment from Black men, the athletes, scholars, and common everyday folks. We can only achieve a new direction if we find the love of self. With that love we discover a new strength to take on these battles because we discover the God within us. One of the finest messages ever delivered to the contemporary Black man comes from a Spike Lee movie, "Get on the Bus." When the character Jeremiah, played by Ossie Davis, has a fatal heart attack, the men, who have come all the way from Los Angeles by bus for the Million Man March, are all quite depressed. It is at that point that George the bus driver (played by Charles Dutton) delivers a message from the God within him, that inner strength. He tells the men,

"We're here because God Almighty wanted us here. And he doesn't care so much about what you already done. God asks what you going to do now...The real march ain't

even started yet. This was only the prelims, the warm up. The real Million Man March won't start until we Black men take charge of our own lives and start dealing with crime, drugs and guns and gangs and children having children and children killing children all across this country. If you all are ready to quit your apathetic and unsympathetic ways as I am and take back control of the Black community. If you're ready to stop being boys...and be the men that our wives, and our mothers and our children are waiting for...and stand up against all the evils lined up against the Black man...and just say we're tired of this shit and we ain't going to take it any more. If you're ready to do that then we got work to do. We've got a lot of work to do."

This is a message that has tremendous importance to every Black man who has abandoned his responsibility to the Black community. We are the trustees of a great asset. That asset is our children. Just as we protect our material assets it is now time for us to protect our human assets. We must begin to give them direction and strength built on the God within, and not support mega churches that treat us much like our ancestors were treated in Fort Jesus, absent the physical torture. But we are prisoners of the doctrine that we can only find salvation through a man who stands in front of us every Sunday and purports to deliver a message from God, when the message of God is within each of us. Seek it out and put your confidence that He will deliver for you if you only act upon His will.

Chapter Seven

SHIP OF ZION

Indeed we put bits in horses' mouths that they may obey us, and we turn their whole body, look also at ships, although they are so large and are driven by fierce winds they are turned by a very small rudder whenever the pilot desires.
James 3 vs. 3-4

Today, Rodger Goodell is the pilot of the Ship of Zion. The National Football League is the largest slave ship known to mankind, because it is the sport that sets the example for all other franchises within that industry. The NFL is the wealthiest league the world has ever known. And it functions within the boundaries of the richest country the world has ever known. Football stadiums across America resemble the slave ships of old. If you place the two side by side, they will parallel each other. Metaphorically, stadiums and ships have the same meaning for the football player and the slave; they both are placed at the bottom and the master is still looking down at them. In the hole of the slave ship the captured African was forced to survive the harrowing three week trip through the "middle passage." They were forced to a prone position in complete darkness at the bottom of the ship for three weeks. So when the hatch door opened they would look up as light beamed down on them. Rations would then be thrown down to the half-starved captives. They believed the food was manna from Heaven, and the light provided them with new energy and hope. The evil and despicable men who tossed the food down into the hole were considered masters from Heaven ordained by God. *"Yet He gave a command to the skies above and opened the doors of the Heavens; He rained down manna for the people to eat, he gave them the grain of Heaven. Men ate the bread of angels; He sent them all the food they could eat." (Psalms 78 verses 23-25*

The same evil doers who put the slaves on the ships, places the athlete in the stadiums. The slavers always piled the slave in the bottom of the ship for the sole purpose of sustaining and increasing the master's wealth. The NFL owners also place the modern day slave on the football field for his economic benefit. *"He shall be like a tree planted by the rivers of water that brings forth its fruit in its season. Whose leaf shall not wither and whatever he does shall prosper. (Psalms 1 verse 3).* Unlike the slave in the cotton field, the football player does not recognize his exploitation. All athletes who find themselves on the world stage in front of 80,000 screaming fans are drunk from the adulation. They know sports would be their destiny, their reason for living. The Black athlete becomes angry when compared to a slave from the past. After all he is the star and he dictates his destiny; he is in charge. The Black athlete does not want to answer the tough question and that is who put him on that football field, basketball court, or baseball diamond? It is the owners who have placed them there and it is the owners who can take it all away. I watched many talented Black players released from their team after a few good years and shipped off to the Canadian Football League. Black players must always be on top of their game, clearly superior to white players who are always given more time to hone their talent. They are seldom shipped off to that other league. During the ugly years of slavery, when a master no longer could use a slave they were forced to leave the plantation and live in the surrounding woods and sometimes swamps. They were on their own and had to survive as best they could. The slave exists for the profits of the owner, and once he costs more to keep than what he can produce he has to go. Correspondingly, the football slave also exists for the profits of his owner and when he is no longer profitable he is released into the woods of the Canadian Football League where he is often treated as a has been who is overworked and underpaid. In the Canadian Football League, many players are acting just like fools and never really enjoy playing in the north because they are constantly trying to get back into the National Football League. In the past I have told some of these men, "why attempt doing something the same way as in the past when you know you're going to have the same result?" Their problem is that they believed they were in control of their own destiny but, in reality, were not. When a slave was traded from one plantation to another, he couldn't just jump up and leave his new master because he liked the old one better. He was not in control of his own destiny. These same players who complain that they got a raw deal from their owners, I also say to them, "the owners and the coaches that took your job away from you are still there in authority. So what makes you believe so strongly that they are going to change their minds about you? Your fate is in their hands." The masters of the Ship of Zion have made a decision, and just like the slave, the player must live with it.

Now on the other hand, the master and his henchmen are not subjected to the same kind of treatment as the players. Coaches, general managers and presidents of the team are immune from the harsh treatment the players suffer. It is a fact that coaches may get fired, but they always seem to end up on another team, either as the new head coach or as an assistant. You seldom read of an NFL coach having to go all the way to Canada in order to stay within his profession. Coach Norv Turner has held head coaching jobs with the Washington Redskins, Oakland Raiders, and now San Diego Chargers. He was also assistant coach with the Dallas Cowboys. Dick Vermeil coached the Philadelphia Eagles, St. Louis Rams, and the Kansas City Chiefs with only one super bowl victory. Pete Bethard has been general manager of a number of NFL teams, and probably would be welcomed at many others if the opportunity arose. Joe Gibbs took a ten year vacation from coaching and was welcomed back to the Washington Redskins when he got bored with racing cars. He retired again, but if he so desired another team would undoubtedly pick him up. Icons of the coaching profession like Vince Lombardi and George Allen landed coaching jobs even after their good years were gone

James Hasty, a former Kansas City Chief cornerback, wrote about the good "ole boy" system in the *Kansas City*

Star in August 2001, after he had been cut from the team because of his high salary. He wrote, "Loyalty can be a great thing in pro sports. It can unify a team and create good chemistry. But the kind of loyalty being practiced in Kansas City will attribute to many losses in the near future if something isn't done soon." Hasty went on to explain that an appointment to the Chief's coaching staff was a prime example of the good "ole boy" system and how treatment of the slaves is different from the various masters. The Chief's president and general manager, Carl Peterson, a former assistant to Dick Vermeil at UCLA and personnel director with the Philadelphia Eagles, repaid Vermeil who had gotten him into the pro ranks of management. He gave St. Louis high draft picks for Vermeil's services, and then rewarded him with a three year contract worth ten million dollars. They had to cut an outstanding football player with much talent left because of his high dollar salary and then turned around and gave it to a mediocre coach.

Vermeil's first move as head coach of the Chiefs was to reward his friend and former Rams assistant, Al Saunders, with the offensive coordinator's job. Vermeil and Saunders quickly agreed that they'd like to pursue a quarterback who would be familiar with their high flying offensive system. A first round draft pick was shipped to St. Louis for Vermeil's old quarterback Trent Green. Hasty concluded by saying, "Do you notice a pattern here? Friends are "hooking up" friends. It is the good 'ole boy's' system and consists primarily of white slave owners and slave drivers." Instead of choosing coaches on a buddy system, the system must change. Coaches should be like political candidates and have to seek out the votes of the players, who would then make the final decision. If the players want to put an end to this, they must get off the Ship of Zion. They must boycott the system and demand changes. In unison, they should pick a Sunday to demonstrate their seriousness and, when the whistle is blown to go pick the "massa's" cotton, they should stage a sit-in inside the locker room. But these strong athletic warriors will shrivel up like spineless cowards if you suggest they take such a strong stand for their freedom. The master syndrome is alive and well in the minds of athletes on the football fields across this country.

A part of the Ship of Zion is the practice facility at every NFL location. That facility is influenced by the old massa's big house. The plantation homes are still standing tall in the 21st Century. Big and spacious, the plantation home has a backside view that shows the field hands at work on the playing fields, practicing for an upcoming game. Owners and managers sit in the shade on second and third level balconies watching their field hands sweat and run while they relax, drinking lemonade and ultimately determining the player's future role on the plantation. Once in a while, one of the field hands will stare up at the managers' watching him from above and he feels a need to work harder. He accepts his status when the coach instructs him to "use the back entrance to the facility. We don't want traffic coming through the front doors of the plantation. We, the administrators, will be the privileged ones to enter through the front door." As in days of old, slaves used the back entrance and, today, if you are caught using the front entrance, you will be fined. The administrators park their vehicles right in front of the

BLACK HORSES/WHITE COTTON AND RELIGION

entrance to the plantation, while the slave's parking lot is either on the side or in the back. His car will be towed if he tries to park in a place not permitted for the slaves. You would think that the players would have the privileged parking slots considering they are the ones who will fill up the stadium on game day. The fans come to see the players, not the administrators. In fact, one would think the players would be running the practice facility, but have you ever heard of a slave running a plantation?

Rebellious slaves who challenged the system were often times hung. Today, players are lynched, not physically, but on paper. Every little act of rebellion is recorded and players have rap sheets just like criminals. With high speed internet, their acts of disobedience are sent to every other plantation. They are tagged, labeled and shipped off like a thief in the night. For some odd reason we never hear from them again. Another team will not pick them up even though they might have shown great talent on the field. They were talented, aggressive, and consistent, everything a team could ask for in a player. That is what they were before their careers were cut off like a surgeon cuts off a leg or two for diabetes and that person is never the same again. These players still feel the need to compete. Their peers call and ask, "Why aren't you playing? We need you out here on the battlefield?" But the surgeon has done his work and the player will never play the game he loves again. They got a raw deal and everyone knows it, the players, coaches, and fans, but the surgeon continues to stay in business, cutting off limbs to keep recalcitrant players from the game they were bred to play.

The managers, like plantation owners, recognize the

rigors of playing football and picking cotton can be stressful to the point of endangering the player and the slave. To counter this stress both players and slaves participate in a number of festivities organized by management of the plantations. There would be ceremonies and festivals when "massa" and slave would gather together at year's end to show that they appreciate each other. The "massa" would prepare a gathering, similar to the way NFL teams do after a football season is over. On this festive occasion, the players actually cut their hair, even buy suits like their "massa" so they can feel a sense of acceptance and pride in their appearance. That is how Somerset Place, a North Carolina plantation, was run. Slaves would gather wearing their finest clothes, those suitable to wear in the presence of the "massa." Satisfying the slaves with a party and giving them a sense of equality by allowing them to enter the mansion lessened the chance of a rebellion against their oppressors. However, after the holidays, the slaves would return to wearing their old rags, go back to the cotton fields and into hell's kitchen, but they would constantly remember the good times they had at the festivities inside the big house. It would be a conversation piece until the following year.

Many Black players in the NFL remind me of Old Peter Law, a slave I once read about. Old Peter was considered a hardworking, obedient slave who refused to disobey his "massa." At year's end, during the Christmas holidays, Old Peter would climb the front steps of the big house and shake his "massa's" hand as if he were shaking the hand of Jesus himself. It was a privilege he was allowed only during the festival and he prided himself in the honor of shaking the hand of the man who held his destiny in the palm of that same hand he shook with such pride and joy. If someone held my destiny in the palm of his hand, I would love to shake it and take my destiny back. I believe that is what Old Peter was trying to do.

High-profile and not so high-profile players attend their annual season-ending party and of course the Christmas party. It is a chance to mingle with those in charge of their future on the field. They have now performed for a year on the field, and are anxious to know how the managers feel about them. They meet the owner, shake his hand, and it makes them feel special, especially if they receive a firm handshake in return. They are at Somerset Place, in the mansion and they want to be reassured that their performance in the cotton field was satisfactory. They don't want to be traded or relegated to duty in the Canadian Football League. They have family and investments right in the cities for which they played and don't want to pull up stakes and start all over again. That hand shake is reassuring and awfully important, especially to the borderline player.

No one in any field of work should be so beholden to another individual that he has to do things outside his normal behavior. Players, who must kiss up to the owners, so they won't get shipped out at the end of the year, engage in abnormal behavior. The game, the glory, and the roar of the crowd are more important than their own dignity. We need more heroes like Curt Flood, who refused to be shipped out like a modern day slave. In 1969, the St. Louis Cardinals tried to trade Flood to the Philadelphia Phillies. Aware of the racist reputation of the Phillies' fans, Flood refused to report to Philadelphia. He sued

103

Commissioner Bowie Kuhn and the National Baseball League. In a December 24, 1969 statement, Flood proclaimed that "After twelve years in the major leagues, I do not feel I am a piece of property to be bought and sold irrespective of my wishes. I believe that any system which produces that result violates my basic rights as a citizen and is inconsistent with the laws of the United States and of the several states." Although Flood lost his suit when the United States Supreme Court ruled in favor of Bowie Kuhn, his case eventually led to the eradication of the oppressive reserve clause. Flood is emblematic of what all professional Black athletes should want to emulate. He stood for dignity and pride. His talent shouldn't be something that can be bartered between men who never played the game and never had the talent to do so. Men involved in athletics are not animals or slaves, and should be afforded the same respect as individuals in other professions where they can not be bought and sold without consideration of their own desires.

The Trans Atlantic Slave Trade was undoubtedly the worst crime ever perpetrated on a race of people. It surpasses the Holocaust in its atrocity and the number of murdered people. Over thirteen million Africans died during that terrible time in history. So many bodies were thrown overboard that a school of sharks were known to follow the ships from Africa to America. The ship captains' rules were harsh and could not be challenged. Many of those thirteen million were Africans who defied his rules. The same was true once they were sold to a plantation owner. His rules were like those of the ship captain, harsh and irreversible. Owners and captains would kill slaves in front of hundreds of others in order to send a message, "you bow down to me as a God, or I'll strike you down right here." *He strikes them as wicked men in the open sight of others, because they turned back from him and would not consider his ways. Job 34 verse 26-27.*

NFL Commissioner Goodell has been given the power by the league owners to punish those players who break the rules of the league as well as society. Goodell sits high and looks down at each individual player's behavior. Their conduct is under the microscope. Obviously, the punishment is not nearly as harsh as that inflicted on recalcitrant slaves, but it is punishment nevertheless. I will use four contemporary players to make my point. All four of these players are at the bottom of the ship, stadium, and America. Tank Johnson of the Chicago Bears (now with the Dallas Cowboys) was suspended for eight games for violating probation on a gun charge. Pac Man Jones of the Tennessee Titans (also now with the Dallas Cowboys) has received a year suspension from the league for a number of run-ins with the law, and Chris Henry was suspended for four games for league violations. Finally, all sport fans await the NFL punishment that will be imposed on Michael Vick once he is released from prison. No one can challenge that these players deserved to be sanctioned, but how about Bill Belichick? Doesn't his behavior deserve some kind of sanctions from the commissioner? It appears that when one from the top is caught cheating the rules change. Commissioner Goddell did not suspend him; he fined him and allowed him to stay in his seat of power. He looks at Bill as a brother, not a potentially Black criminal who happens to be in the NFL. Bill Belichick sits high and looks low; he is not under the same rules as the players/slaves. Without a doubt he has done this same thing in the past. This is not a first time offense; he just happened to get caught. *"Be that as it may, I did not burden you nevertheless, being crafty, and I caught you cunning."* 2 *Corinthians, 12 verse 16.*

Coach Belichick is cunning. Cunning means skilled at deceiving people, skillful or clever, craftiness. It seems only fair that if Marion Jones has to give back her medals for cheating, then Coach Belichick should give back his Super Bowl rings. But for Mr. Belichick to give back his rings is equivalent to the United States Government giving the United States back to the Native Americans, because we all know this country was stolen; they were cunning like Belichick. If the sports world and the United States Government are going to crack the whip on the backs of Black athletes, then that same whip should come whistling down on the back of cheaters like Bellichick. But in a world where we know justice is often a stranger, where ethical and moral principles are viewed as a nuisance, and doing the right thing seems wrong and doing wrong is acceptable, we cannot expect the power structure to penalize one of their own in the same manner as the slaves/players. Even more disgusting is that the powers will justify their actions and really believe they are correct. The most powerful nation in the world can attack a small third world country and America celebrates. Our soldiers are considered heroes because they carried out the mission with precision. George Bush stands on a naval ship and in full regalia, declares victory as though this country just defeated a major world power. The slaves confronted overwhelming

106

power when brought to this country. Secretary of Defense Donald Rumsfeld told the entire world that they were about to witness power so awesome that the only possible response would be shock and awe. The same kind of behavior is prevalent among the owners, coaches and managers of the NFL. They love to keep their players in a state of shock and awe so they will follow orders like soldiers on the battlefield and slaves in the cotton fields. I believe the NFL is so popular because it is a mirror image of a society that measures value based on power and not love. There is very little compassion for the weak and timid on the football fields of America, and there is very little compassion on the streets of America or in the halls of Congress and the West Wing of the White House.

A thief is a person who steals another's property. The European was a thief; he not only stole people from a continent, in the process they occupied and raped that same continent and on the way destroyed a mighty culture. The thief has no emotional connection with what he steals, destroys, and kills, because he is not operating from any kind of moral compass. The thief operates from an amoral and greed inspired perspective. The keepers of wealth are cunning; they rape a country of its wealth in natural and human resources, and do nothing to help rebuild that country. The same happens to athletes who come from the inner-cities of America. In professional sports, the Black athletes' abilities, athleticism, and speed are more valuable than his person. The owners get rich off the Black athlete just as the slave owner got rich of the strength of the African. The keepers of wealth dedicate their lives to preserving the imbalance of wealth throughout the world because they believe in their divine right, the order of things, to keep wealth out of the hands of the exploited. The problem is the hands that get dirty are exploited and make the wealth for the hands that stay clean.

This is a crucial time in history where we must no longer succumb to those who have placed themselves in power. To the contrary, we must now empower ourselves. For the fruits that we bear can sustain us if we lean on God and ask Him to be our salvation, through a realization of the God within ourselves. If the people, who find themselves living on the bottom of the slave ship today, continue to live their lives the same way, not recognizing the power within, those from above will continue to feed them an unhealthy philosophy of life. *Psalm 80 Verse 5* tells us, *"You have fed them with the bread of tears, and given them tears to drink in great measure."*

For all my Christian friends and the millions of others living in the 7th millennium and waiting for the return of the Messiah, this seems like the right time. The conditions are perfect for him to return and bring in a new world. The question to be asked is whether Jesus will destroy the current system and bring in the new Jerusalem, a new mind-set, new ideas of fair and honest living not for a few, but for the millions? This time the slaves will share in the glory. *"For we have heard him say that this Jesus of Nazareth shall destroy this place, and shall change the customs which Moses delivered to us. Acts 6 verse 14.*

Many tears are shed during the off season in the NFL. Favorite players, claiming to have so much knowledge and insight on life, seem to fall so easily to the temptations of life. Knowledge is the awareness gained through experience.   Character is a quality that separates one person from another.   When we govern our lives based on knowledge there should be a keen awareness of those things that are right, fair and just.   If character is not added into the equation then we live as infidels.   A nation can possess character and knowledge.   When it does then that country will seek peace and not war, it will be concerned about the economic, physical, and psychological security of all its people, not just the upper class.   Every great nation that portrayed a solid foundation of character and knowledge, lasted thousands of years, other nations that lacked those qualities was equivalent to a flashy and loud athlete; they come with ability but leave with apathy.

Whether in life or football, everything comes to an end and a new beginning will emerge.   One may find they are ending a ten-year marriage or a ten year professional career and they may face depression and sadness for a time until that something new comes along.   When I finished my 11 year run in professional football, I had to admit I was somewhat shocked for a moment, until that same energy, passion, determination and courage I played with on the grid iron reasserted itself through my pen.   Now I have the most intriguing, philosophical and spiritual feeling about my writing and my new publications.   I am a giant among men, and my pen is more powerful, influential, and inspiring than any sport event.   We can be at our lowest point in life, and still climb to our greatest heights.

I may be wrong, but living in America I have the right to speak my mind.   That is a freedom I have and a privilege I will exercise.   There are many ships afloat on the ocean of our minds, where decisions must be made.   The problem is many do not feel they have the power to make the tough decisions; they have settled for others to make them. People and athletes get tossed around like a wet dish rag because we find our lives are in somebody else's hands opposed to our own. I encourage every strong-minded person to learn how to swim so they can decide whether to jump ship or stay on board. I have chosen to jump off the Ship of Zion and swim to shore. I will build my own ship, not a replica of the old but rather a prototype for the future, "The Ship of Freedom." Eventually we all reach a point in life where we wake up to a new dawn and choose a better life for ourselves more fulfilling than the old. It will be a life predicated on living for ourselves rather than for others. Life is short, the ocean is huge and if you find yourself afloat on a ship not of your choosing, you will miss out on the abundance of what the world has to offer you. *"By the rivers of Babylon there we sat down, yeah, we wept when we remembered Zion. We hung our harps upon the willows in the midst of it for there those who carried us away captive and asked of us a song. And those who plundered us requested mirth, saying, 'sing us one of the songs of Zion.'" Psalm 137 verse 1-3.*

Chapter Eight

LEVELING THE PLAYING FIELD

"Why didn't God solve the problems in the beginning?" —AP

God has given us free will to create a path through life of our own choosing, which includes working out the problems that we create, along the way. As human beings we seem to play a game with God. We conduct our lives in such a way that we create overwhelming problems, then turn to Him in prayer to rescue us from our own stupidity. Essentially, we waste time and energy waiting on the God of the universe to intervene and relieve us of a burden we drummed up on our own. In reality, God has given us all free choice to mess up and, therefore, gives us the same freedom to work it out. There comes a time in life when you start applying your sound knowledge and start acting like an adult and not a child. In *1 Corinthians 13 vs. 11*, the Good Book tells us "When I was a child I spoke as a child, I understood as a child, I thought as a child; but when I became a man, I put away childish things."

All the Black parents who, today, have young men involved in sports must be aware of the traps that can lie in front of the athlete. Parents must understand that athletics is not necessarily based on ability, but politics and favoritism. These negative intrusions are destroying the good name of football and basketball, in the 21st Century. The parent and the athlete are often taken on an emotional roller coaster by coaches at the high school and college level, who promise so much but deliver so little.

When we examine pro football and how unbalanced it is in treatment of the players involved, we must first examine the seed planted in the minds of the young ones who are recruited to play this brutal sport. The young athlete may have a few good games, show some promise for the future, and then the coach will plant the seed of greatness in the heads of the parents. Excited over the prospect of their child doing great things, matching Michael Jordan in basketball skills and Michael Vick in football, they begin to put posters of those exceptionally great players on the wall of the child's rooms, planting in his mind that is what he will become someday. The parents then begin to believe in the lie and, of course, the child is sold on a great future.

The first job of a parent should be to reveal to the child the facts about professional sports. The fact being that only the few will be chosen to play. The parent should say to the child, "If you want to be a professional football player in the National Football League, here are the facts;

Every year over 1 million boys play high school football

The same year only 55,000 of that 1 million will play in college

13,000 actually get football scholarships

The NFL will scout approximately 6,000 of that 55,000

340 from that group will be invited to the NFL combine

320 of that 340 will actually sign NFL contracts

After 4 years of playing in the NFL roughly 140 of that 320 will still be playing, and less than 100 will be Black."

"Millions will dream, thousands will sacrifice and only a few will become a Pro." —A.P.

I believe every man, woman, and child should dream so big that even if they do not reach their desired goal, they will get at least a piece of it. Not everybody is going to become a doctor, lawyer, nurse, accountant, astronaut or professor. These professionals require special licenses, a college education, specialized training, testing, and years of study. But they will survive in a competitive society because they have mind power. Men and women with mind power last over 30 or more years in their craft. On the other hand, you have professional athletes, singers, actors, artists, and writers working in professions that do not require a college degree, only thick skin and tons of confidence. Many start out believing they can make it in these fields, but fall short due to inconsistency, apathy, and a lack of determination.

"God doesn't gain from human suffering, only
humans gain from another human's misery." —-AP

This past year, in 2007 during football season, I witnessed the kind of pain and suffering created by a combination of parental anxiety and the hypocrisy of those men who coach the young. As a speed coach, athletic consultant, writer and philosopher, I wear many hats. I also get the opportunity to advise and counsel many parents and young athletes concerning their future in sports. I had a single mother (single mothers are usually the norm) call me about the unfair treatment her son was receiving at the hands of his coach. This young man was only ten and played in the pee wee league. The young boy was fast, agile, and had the spirit to be a real team player. He played very consistent, possessed a great attitude but the coach had many friends with sons on the team. Three other boys played the same position as the young boy. When the team was losing and needed someone to spark the team to victory, they would put Renee's son in the game to run the ball. But if they were winning, friendship took precedence and Renee's son just sat and watched. Even though the parents in the stands knew Renee's son was the better player, they remained silent while their sons dominated the time on the field. This is called favoritism and is destroying competitive sports in America. The seed of favoritism is planted early in the minds of the young players. A bad experience, like the one Renee's son encountered playing the game he loved and was very good at, can destroy a young mind and kill the drive to be the best. There is only one way to eliminate favoritism, and that is to get rid of the people in charge and bring in a new system that is fair and reasonable and will encourage all children.

"Create a life of your choosing." —AP

High School Horror:

There are some coaches in High school that spit venom all day, week, month, and year. These unfair coaches are good for absolutely nothing. Their motives are simple, to make the lives of some athletes miserable and others a pleasurable experience. I am thankful that my father was my coach during pee wee league and in high school my head coach was fair, which allowed me to go to the next level with little interruption. Some of the more disdainful comments made by coaches are: "He has a bad attitude," or "He's a thug," also "He's un-coachable," or my favorite, "He's all mouth." Coaches use these derogatory comments all the time to describe players they do not want to see go to the next level. They literally tell college scouts these lies when the latter come to scout certain players. You have coaches lying through their teeth and heart, because they are jealous when they see proud parents supporting their gifted child. They deliberately try to destroy that kind of bonding between parent and child, because the core of the coach's soul is rotten, like road kill on a Sunday afternoon.

A much more tragic story happened to a young high school athlete, who played football, basketball, baseball,

115

and also ran track. This was the kind of young man who dominated any sport in which he participated. He especially shined in football like the sun breaking through thunder clouds on a rainy day. He had the physical body of a grown man and the mature and discipline attitude like a well respected Marine sergeant. For some odd reason, during his junior year, his coach decided not to play him, not for disciplinary reasons, but just because he could. I received a call from his father who asked for advice on how to handle the situation. I replied in anger and raw emotions, "Got damn it, not again. Not another potentially great athlete being screwed over by a weak ass jealous coach," I whispered to myself. After calming down I instructed the father to go to the school and "kick the coach's ass right in front of the whole school and the entire football team." We laughed momentarily because sometimes we have to laugh to keep from actually hurting someone. I have heard it said, "We laugh to keep from crying," but I think for many of us we are cried out and want more than just tears. We need the judgment of God's angels to come down and destroy these people who destroy innocent young minds. I attended the next game sitting right next to the father. I watched as the man, definitely in pain, stared down at his son on the sidelines. The son would occasionally make eye contact with his father and shrug his shoulders in confusion. We all glared in shock as we watched an inferior athlete; playing the position his son dominated a year before. I literally experienced the slow demise of a young talented man whose dreams were lost because of an insensitive and jealous coach.

The following day, the father of the young athlete

had a meeting with the coach concerning his son's playing time. The coach became irate and scowled, "Look, if you don't like my style take your son off my team and transfer him somewhere else." Shocked and in disbelief the father called me at a loss as to what action he should take. In the meantime his son was losing interest in sports, and appeared to be suffering from depression. We examined the options open to the young man; he was a junior and if he transferred, he wouldn't be able to play his senior year. Basically his high school football career would be over because when you transfer you lose a year of eligibility. That same year the young boy's grade point average dropped from 3.8 to 2.1, his love of sports faded away like a butterfly on a spring morning, and his mood became very defiant. After graduation he signed up for the football team at the community college, but dropped out before the end of the semester. He is now living with his girlfriend, who works at the local Wal-Mart. He spends his time drinking with his old friends who never had a shot at college ball and possibly greatness. On the weekends they get loud and talk about what could have been as he grabs old letters from colleges that recruited him. He received letters from outstanding Division One schools such as University of Southern California, University of California at Los Angeles, Norte Dame and University of Michigan. That is all that is left of his dream, old outdated letters. His drinking, boisterous loud talk and his disappointment have left him in a constant state of depression, and a deep, abiding dislike for a high school coach who wrecked his potentially successful career.

      I constantly advise parents to investigate the coach

in whose hands they place their child's future. If you allow a potentially racist and incompetent man to have that kind of control over your son, without first investigating his character and coaching ability, the child receives the blunt of your error. For the most part coaches do not care about your child's future, only wins and losses. You, as a parent, must change your perception of the coach. We must do a better job of preparing our young for the potential lies that coaches will tell them just for the purpose of exploiting their talents.

What we need is a new paradigm from which our community functions. Presently we look to sports as our salvation, the means by which we can escape the inner city blues. But that must change. We have to build our communities around reading and writing not running fast, singing well, and jumping high. When you change the landscape of your mind no one can come into your life with lies and empty promises. The father who called me about his son and the mother about her son, made the error of trusting the men who claim to be able to help their children reach the next level of excellence. A young man's grade point average went from a 3.8 to a 2.1 in one semester all because of a coach who never played professional football, and only wanted to live vicariously through the other children. It is similar to you placing your child's life in the hands of a healer who cannot heal.

The question that now confronts us is how to help a young athlete who is mentally crippled because sports did not live up to what it promised. They have been inundated with misinformation. To them sports is like Heaven. But what they do not realize is that Heaven is a place of balance, order, and godliness. Athletics is a place where you experience favoritism, racism and politics. Because the leaders at the top do not play fair, the entire industry is out of balance. Whether you are an athlete or not, if the top of the structure is not leveled, eventually it will crumble; nations, empires, kingdoms, companies, franchises, and families have come to ruin because of an imbalance. It is like having five teenage children and they all spend the same amount of time in the field working, but you pay all of them differently for doing the same thing. How can they feel good about themselves or how can you maintain a united front if they all know some are making more than others? This mentality of lying, cheating, not treating all players equal is damaging to our communities and our children. Therefore, I maintain that sports should be banned from the Black community for at least a ten year period so we can revive our children's minds, remove the illusion of sports, and recapture their souls from the damage that has been done over the years, due to placing their hopes in a false prophet of success.

"Parents show up at games, not classrooms where the real games are being played."—AP

Long Beach Poly High School in Southern California has produced more NFL players than any other high school in the United States. I think that is a great honor because it shows that the coach's philosophy works for a great number of athletes at the school. However, what about the athletes that do not make it to the next level? Do they continue with their life and education or does life seem to fall by the way side when their dreams of athletic stardom die? The primary reason why young Black athletes suffer when sports fail to live up to their expectations is because they expect too much from sports. The young idealistic athlete doesn't recognize that sports will always take more than it gives. Football not only takes physical health from the individual, it can also rob a person of their mental and spiritual being. There are high schools that win state championships, but lose their accreditation all in the same year. What kind of society places physical play over a healthy education? It is called "Moral Decay."

Black athletes expect to get something out of sports. They are: 1) Money, 2) Prestige, 3) Fames, 4) Glory, 5) Accolades, 6) Championships, 7) Records, 8) Material Possessions, 9) Escape, and 10) Confidence.

The average white high school player also will not make it to the National Football League. But instead, he will become an engineer, lawyer, doctor, scientist, and teacher. Unlike Blacks, white athletes play for the enjoyment of the sport, not as a means of escape. The white athlete grows up knowing that he does not need sports to survive in America, his country built on the back of African slave labor. He does not need the NFL, NBA, MLB or AFL, he has America, which includes the constitution, the government, the military and Christianity. The Black athlete, on the other hand, needs the NFL because he has been sold athletic dreams his entire life. Because he has become dependent on sports he believes that he must kiss the ring of the king, the coaches and owners in the NFL. What he fails to recognize is that sports would be void of excitement, action, and intensity without the Black athlete. The NFL can only be maintained through the speed, agility, and athleticism of the Black horse, Black slave, Black Negro, Black n-----r, and Black athlete. He has been running in America since the Mayflower anchored on these shores.

"When Jesus saw that the people came running together, he rebuked the unclean spirit saying to it, "Deaf and dumb spirit I command you come out of him and enter him no more!" Mark 9:25

We must be liberated from the "deaf and dumb spirit." Concerning sports today, God does not ordain unhealthy actions to glorify His name. Sports in America should not be a means of escape from poverty and hardship. This is the richest country the world has ever known and there should be no ghettoes in America. But as long as the distribution of wealth is allocated unevenly, there will be an inordinate number of Black people living in a state of abject poverty. That is exactly why it upset me when I saw the evangelical ministers come into our locker room and hustle a portion of the pay from predominantly Black ball players. Instead of lining the pockets of these charlatans, the players should give that same money to deserving children and families in the inner cities. In Malachi, God does not direct the people to give tithes to jack-legged preachers, but to the poor. The poor can be found in any major city where these very ball players make their living. They should be giving back to the community, not to some building encased in gold. Humanitarian acts must be acted out where there is the biggest need. But most of our heroes in America have taken away from humanity, rather than preserving it and/or giving to it.

Contained Commodities:

The most powerful and influential commodity in the sports world today are the legs of the Black athlete. His speed and agility have electrified crowds for decades. In the 1936 Olympics, America used the legs of Jesse Owens to bring glory and supremacy to America. As Hitler sat in the stands confident that the superior Aryan race would prevail in track, Owens embarrassed the racist dictator by not only winning the 100 yard dash once, but twice after the Nazis leader contested his first victory. In 1946 when the boring all-white NFL was forced to re-integrate, because they did not want to compete against the all Black Professional Football League, they took the legs of the Black athlete to breathe new life into a dying sport. Beginning with Marion Motley, and going forward from Jim Brown, Gayle Sayers, Walter Payton, Emmit Smith and today, a young Reggie Bush, Black running backs have been the fuel that drives the offensive game in football. And let's not forget the late and great Jackie Robinson, who revolutionized the game of baseball with his speed, actually stealing home in a 1947 World Series game shocking every baseball fan in America, racist and all. Hertz rental was on the verge of bankruptcy and they grabbed the legs of O.J. Simpson and made him run through airports and jump over rows of seats, like a show horse in competition.

Whether in football, basketball, baseball, track, and even soccer, the surplus value of the richest commodity in sports, the legs of the Black athlete, allows for the weaker vessels on the team to get paid. Those athletes who do not possess the speed benefit from the stronger and more athletic players. During the years of segregated colleges and universities in the south, Black players from those schools would go north to play football. One year, while Bear Bryant was coach at the University of Alabama, he scheduled the University of Southern California (USC) to play his team right there in Alabama. That was the year USC's running back was Sam Cunningham. He had a field day running around and sometimes through the Alabama defense. They easily defeated a good Alabama team and Coach Bryant had made his point to the thousands of alumni who watched that slaughter. They all recognized that it was the superior speed of the Blacks that defeated their beloved Alabama. Soon after that, Alabama recruited its first Black ball players and they haven't looked back since.

Realize there is an economic imbalance when a weaker athlete gets paid the same amount as the stronger one. This is an economic fact and it is not right. It is not only the weaker athlete that has benefited from the superior speed and ability of the Black man, but the entire country. The motion, the muscles, and the legs are needed for economic purposes:

To build America	you need legs to work.
To fight wars	you need legs to fight.
To win Super Bowls	you need legs to run.
To win Olympics	you need legs to jump.
To win championships	you need legs to win.

There are many athletes that do not possess the gift of leg strength and speed to win alone, to compete alone, to fight alone, run alone, jump alone and have the self-confidence to be alone. But on the other hand, they have what the Black athlete does not and that is power, private property, industry, wealth, influence and decision making authority. They also control the richest commodity in the sports industry, the legs of the Black athlete. The man cracks the whip and the Black athlete runs fast, jumps high, and essentially sacrifices his dignity for the glory of being on the football field, and the money that allows him to buy the next Mercedes Benz, Jaguar, or BMW. For that, he overlooks or turns his head when the weaker athlete is paid as much or sometimes more than him.

What If I helped a man build the most beautiful house in the world and when the house was finished, I was kicked out for no apparent reason. I was not even offered a spare room, couldn't use the bathroom or get within a 50 yard radius of the house. And every time I would look at the house it made me angry. When the unpaid labor force experiences this type of injustice, they have a right to tear the house down and burn it. *Jeremiah 18, verse 7-8 tells us, "If at any time I announce that a nation or kingdom is to be uprooted, torn down and destroyed, and if that nation I warned repents of its evil, then I will relent and not inflict on it the disaster I had planned."*

Fair Game:

The changing of the oceans' currents can take you in directions not of your choosing. It is my responsibility to light that path and take you in the direction of self-discovery, not the path of the opposition. They have you believing that sports is bigger than you, when in actuality, you are the sports industry. Without you (the Black athlete) she would fall to her knees. However, today she stands and will continue to as long as your distant perception of what sports is about stays the same. The hero mentality in sports is crippling the industry as well. We grew up watching Spiderman, Superman, and Batman as our heroes. They are super stars, and everyone wants to be like them and achieve stardom playing a team sport. I can not fix the sports industry's problems within these pages. It will take much more. As Black athletes we have lived up to our commitment to the industry, but it has not delivered for us what we deserve. But as Nina Simone sings, *"A new day is coming."* And that new day is about leveling the playing field.

"You're a better man first before you become a great athlete."—AP

We need a new order in the sports world, something we can call "Athletic Order." Without that order we fail collectively. When you view the entire universe, you see the order of God. The sun, earth and moon have always been in harmony. A complete human being or athlete must realize that without a relationship to the natural order of things, we are:

Unbalanced
Incomplete
Lacking

125

LEVELING THE PLAYING FIELD

Unsure
Doubtful
Fearful
Afraid
Uncertain
Indecisive

My method, theory, philosophy, and personal knowledge can not be bought, but it can fix the entire sports industry. We so desperately need real solutions, tangible methods to uplift the human spirit. We need models of hope, past and present, to give more than just talk and politics. We need to know what inspired a Curt Flood and what happened to Michael Vick. People love to talk about those things they seek to achieve. That is why Sunday church services are so crowded; people come together to talk about Heaven because they are living in hell. I have known Heaven to be a place of order, fairness and balance. We find in *Luke 11 verse 2* the following, "So he said to them, 'When you pray, say, *our father in Heaven, hallowed be your name. Your kingdom come, your will be done on earth as it is in Heaven.*"

Why do we choose to live in hell on earth and God tells us of a Kingdom that is not out of reach. Do people really want Heaven on earth, do people really believe in the Gospel of Jesus? Look at yourself, and look at the people that surround you. Look at the people at your job you hate so much, look at your partner who you spend so much time with and ask do you love that person? Look at your clothes, look at how you eat, and what you eat, and take a look at your habits. Are they habits of Heaven or hell? You must define your life and know you crave Heaven and you must eliminate hell.

The hell that needs to change in the sports industry starts off with the coaches, who have personal agendas to destroy young, gifted Black and white athletes. Changing this vital element is crucial because they are the ones who teach, direct, coach, and motivate our young to either go beyond their expectations of greatness or end up becoming victims. Coaches must be held to very high standards of excellence or there will never be a solution to this apathy and athletic decay. The same high standards the coach is being held to must also apply to the athlete's work ethic, attitude, morality and integrity. When young people can not measure the positive results of hard, honest work and dedication in the form of awards and honors, they will be ill prepared, once they enter the professional sports industry, to achieve excellence in the above listed values.

Leveling the playing field-

There is only one way to level the playing field in the National Football League and that is through a revision of the pay scale. Essentially, players need to earn what they make. Aside from his early endorsements, Tiger Woods did not earn any money until he finished high enough in a tournament to get paid. Serena and Venus Williams became millionaires by winning tournaments on the tennis court. In other words, they proved themselves in their particular sport. In football, there are too many millionaires before they played their first game as a professional. These players come out of college, get as high as fifty million dollar contracts, and haven't even tried on the uniform or seen a play book. Soon we will watch as the NFL sign young kids still in the pee wee league to lucrative contracts based on their promise of future greatness. Whatever happened to the old concept of earning your way to the top?

Under my slotting system you will have players who understand the team concept and are not lost in the "me first" attitude, that is so pervasive in the NFL now. You will have more efficient players, less injuries, and better teams. Money affects people differently when they have to earn it. You are more energized and determined to prove your worth, so that you can get paid. Money given to players prior to the season is equivalent to a free lunch, which tends to spoil 95% of athletes. Realize that with ten million dollars after taxes in the bank, before earning it, athletes are more prone to fake an injury. During my eleven year professional career I had to earn every penny and then some, but I played hard and injured. I played with some "pink dress wearing athletes," crying over something as irrelevant as a hang nail. Ask yourself, if you were coming straight out of college earning thirty million dollars, would you fake a few injuries in order to miss a couple pre-season games and a couple regular season games, if you had no chance of making the playoffs? Fake injuries happen on a daily basis on practically every team. This cheating the system can be eliminated if the NFL used my system of play for pay.

An additional change is also necessary in order to level the playing field. The teams must begin to reward players who perform and penalize those that do not. Under my system, a starter would find himself as a backup, or on the practice squad, with their pay being significantly reduced for many different reasons, from poor performance to injury or being outplayed by another player. Imagine a back-up player, who is earning $500,000, all of a sudden is elevated to the starting position, which has a salary of 4 million dollars, and you don't even have to write up a new contract. This will bring the work ethic back to the game, and players will not sit out games for hang nails, or other trivial reasons. Team performance throughout the entire sports industry will improve because every dime will be earned. This is the American way—the pursuit of athletic glory and financial payoff through hard work. Through the slotting system, an athlete's money is earned and championships are won. Below is an example of the slotting system pay scale:

Offensive starters will all be paid a base salary of $4,000,000 a year or $250,000 a game.
Offensive backup's will be paid a base salary of $1,000,000 a year or $62,500 a game.

Defensive starters will all be paid a base salary of $4,000,000 a year or $250,000 a game.

Defensive backup's will all be paid a base salary of $1,000,000 a year or $62,500 a game.

Kickers and punters will all be paid a base salary of $1,000,000 a year or $62,500 a game.

Game day players on the roster that are not starters

will all be paid $1,000,000 a year or $62,500 a game.

Practice squad players' base salary will be $500,000 a year or $31,250 a game.

There are nine reasons why the slotting system is good for sports.

When an athlete is drafted out of college or high school, whether they are the first taken or the last chosen, they will not expect a hand out based on past performances. Teams will not be giving out truck loads of money in the form of signing bonuses. Athletes will be given the opportunity to earn their wealth, depending on where they slot from week to week, either as a starter, a back up, or a practice squad player.

Drafted or non-drafted players will be able to receive money from endorsements, and other outside affiliates.

Every athlete that signs a contract will be under that contract for a period of no longer than four years, equivalent to a presidential term. After four years, all players will become free agents and part of the annual draft all over again.

College players, who will be eligible for the draft after their senior year, will also be eligible, but must compete against the current players no longer under contract.

No back door dealings. All teams will have an opportunity to allocate players through draft and trade.

Trading players under contract will happen for one

month out of the year, after the draft.

Throughout the entire process, with the draft and trade, there is no money exchanged, only after games are the athletes rewarded.

There will be no more privileges given to average athletes. Every athlete will actually have to play to be paid, according to where they slot from week to week.

Owners and administrators will not have to worry about cap room to pay a particular player. Every dime of their $116,500,000 will be spent fairly and evenly for every player.

To level the playing field financially in the National Football League and throughout the entire sports world, would be the greatest accomplishment in athletics since the First Modern Olympiad held in Athens, Greece in 1896. Why does the playing field need to be leveled? The answer is quit obvious and that is to eliminate some of the ills in the sports industry, which are a reflection of our society as a whole. Just as there is an unequal distribution of the wealth in the larger society, the same holds true of the NFL and other team sports. There needs to be a much more equal distribution of the wealth in this country through redistribution. Dr. WEB DuBois put it best when he wrote, "The ideal of poverty... this is the direct antithesis of the present American ideal of Wealth. We cannot all be wealthy. We should not all be wealthy. In an ideal industrial organization, no person should have an income which he does not personally need; nor wield a power solely for his own whim. If civilization is to turn out millionaires, it will also turn out beggars and prostitutes...A simple healthy life on limited income are the only responsible ideal of civilized folk." Not only must we level the playing field in sports, but we must do the same in the real world where people suffer unnecessarily because the playing field for survival in America has never been level. If we are to survive as a civilization it must be done.

Chapter Nine:

THE PHILOSOPHY OF ATHLETICS

*"Theory and life had become fused into a single reality for
me, and neither made sense without the other."* —
Dr. Harry Edwards

I am grateful to all the players throughout my
career who have taken time, before and after practice, to
help improve my athletic skills and increase my value as a
player. Their help allowed me to stay in the game for many
years. I offer a special thanks to the coaches that had the
patience to also help in my development on the "field of
dreams."

It has been seven years sine I started writing and
talking about sports, essentially sharing my philosophy on
the sports industry in America. I am tired of seeing young,
gifted men lose their self-worth when their dreams of a
professional career in sports comes crumbling down. It is
also frustrating to watch when young men also lose
direction in their lives and recede into a state of depression
when trying to make the transition from dreams of an
athletic career to the nightmare that they must seek
another skill and are not compared to so. If these young

people do not begin to prepare early for the strong possibility that they will not make it to the top of the mountain of sports, then they will die with old shoes on their feet. For these reasons I have made the decision to step out on faith and elevate myself to a position of influence and leadership in the struggle to expose the sports world for what it really is. You cannot wait on freedom, but must raise yourself to the level of being free by taking bold steps against those who would constantly oppress you for their own profits and control. The basis for my assertion of leadership is experience. Our problem today is that we have too many so-called leaders and teachers claiming to be experts on subjects, problems, and issues they have never experienced. Please don't misunderstand what I am trying to convey. There are millions of people who have captivating thoughts and thousands are compelled to act based on their ideas. But the real benefit to society and others comes from those who have actual experience; that should be our motivating force today. We cannot afford to be guided by people that continue to disappoint us because of their lack of experience in any given field in which they claim expertise. You can view the ocean from a comfortable distance, but until you actually get into the water and experience its exhilarant feeling against your skin, you will never know the magic the ocean carries hidden deep in its depth. The ocean will remain just a large body of water viewed from the limited vision of your eyes. You develop a clearer image once you submerge your body into the water. Then you can make an account of how the water affects you internally. The Black athlete is on trial today in America. His self image has been defined through media bashing. Many athletes come from humble beginnings. Many look to sports as their savior. These feelings are formed at a young age. Some grow up convinced that without sports, they cannot succeed in life. They believe that without sports they cannot rise above their condition of hunger, poverty, and illiteracy. They are constantly searching for the adulation and confirmation that they are good from all the wrong people. That is why many Black athletes will risk the safety of their bodies to get in the game and perform at a level to satisfy their coach and the crowd. But what they do not understand is that the coach and the crowd are looking for reasons to put the athlete down. It is a love/hate relationship. The white crowd loves the superb performance of the Black athlete, but they hate the fact that it is a Black man performing these outstanding feats. When that man slips up and fails in their eyes, he is booed and jeered right out of the stadium. Recently, one of the finest young Black athletes to put on a football uniform threw two interceptions in one game and was booed. It caused him to recede into a state of depression. There was talk that, after the game, he had actually put a gun to his head. The young man took these drastic steps, because no one had taught him that it is all right to do badly in life. No one had taught him that he must satisfy himself, find his greatness deep inside his soul and then worry about everyone else. Instead he is looking for praise from Jesus, the coaches and the white crowd. As a result, he then becomes a man allowing the television announcers, the coaches and the crowd to dictate his values, his culture and his self-worth.

THE PHILOSOPHY OF ATHLETICS

What these athletes do not understand is that sports cannot bridge the gap between apparent conflicts that have been around for generations. Conflicts like racism and the hypocrisy that are an intricate part of it, have always existed in American institutions. Regardless of how great the athlete's sports career and championships he may win, he cannot improve his self-image in a sporting arena unless he is willing to give up the man made platform of fame that calls for him to engage in human sacrifice. The owners and coaches do not sacrifice, nor are they criticized in the same manner as the athlete. That is, their integrity or commitment to the game is never challenged. Until the Black athlete comes to understand that he is not going to be treated with the same deference as the coach and the owners, he will continue to suffer these bouts of depression.

So what is it the Black athlete should do to counter this feeling of dependence on people who really do not have his best interest at heart? First, the athlete must understand that he cannot always turn to God to relieve the stress he feels, since God didn't put it there. We Black athletes, past and present, must always keep in mind that our careers are in the hands of men who usually have never been athletes. The athlete cannot allow the un-caring and insensitivity, or often incompetence of a few men to cause him stress to the point that he might do something irrational, like placing a gun to his head. Stress often evolves when one senses a crisis is at hand. A crisis situation is when the event can either make or break you. When the athlete reacts to a crisis situation with the attitude of what can I learn from this, it will give him the strength, knowledge, and wisdom that he never knew he possessed. When you react with fear and uncertainty, a crisis can rob the athlete of his dreams and ultimately kill him. He must call on his strength and wisdom to overcome all crisis situations, The conscientious athlete always comes through in the clutch because of five main reasons: 1) he believes in himself outside the walls of sports, 2) he understands that racism exists in sports, 3) he understands that the best players do not always get to play the game, 4) he understands what it means to practice without pressure, 5) he understands that participating in sports is only one moment in his life.

The Ideological Foundation:

The weak athlete was never meant to be a competitor in the professional world of sports, but as long as power remains in the hands of people who look like him, he shall remain an intricate part of the game. In reality the game of football separates the weak from the strong and in that light 70% of the labor force is Black. Today, the performance of the Black athlete is essential in sustaining the sports industry. Without the Black player's blood and sweat on Sunday afternoon, the NFL would crumble. This is known as plantation capitalism. In the sports industry we have noble principles, but we are seeing practices that cannot be ignored. Without concern for his environment, the owners of these teams, with vast amounts of money, will seek out that young Black who has talent and pull him out of the pathological conditions under which he lives. He will bring him onto the plantation to perform for the economic gain of the owner. They give young men, like LeBron James, lucrative contracts and make certain that all the others know that the same wealth awaits them if only they will develop their athletic skills instead of their mental acumen. It has been planted in the minds of our youth that "without athletics the Black child, living under dire conditions of poverty in the world's richest nation, is nothing and his future is meaningless." As a result, too many young and gifted Black men have tunnel vision when it comes to the NFL and sports, in general. They believe that because they can run, jump, and throw, the industry owes them something. I am reminded of the words of the late Dr. Benjamin E. Mays, "if you are ignorant the world is going to cheat you. If you are weak, the world is going to kick you. If you are a coward, the world is going to keep you running." The Black athlete must ask himself are you running with a purpose, because there has to be meaning for the pain you endure. Young men are not aware of what it takes to make an NFL team. According to the National Federation of State High School Sports Association data, there are over one million high school football players in America every year, that same year there were 54,000 college football players, and only 13,000 received scholarships. Finally, out of the entire number of college players, only 340 get invited to the NFL combine, 320 sign NFL contracts, and only 140 remain in the NFL after four years, with 87 being Black. With these statistics it is apparent the chances of anyone individual making it to the pro's is minimal.

Making it to the NFL is only one end of the spectrum. At the other is getting out of the league with a secure position in the private sector. These opportunities are primarily reserved for the white ballplayers that usually have not been as good as the Blacks and are not the reason for winning Super Bowls, bringing pride to the team and the city. But still, Black ball players walk out of the game with very few opportunities to continue performing in the world of business and industry. The Psalmist in the Bible states, "He shall be like a tree, planted by the rivers of water that bring forth its fruit in its season whose leaf also shall not wither and whatever he does shall prosper." Athletes have dry seasons. They get old, injured and ultimately rejected and often black balled from the sports industry. Like the old slave who labored all his life for the master and then is put out in the woods to die, the Black professional football player is put out to just fade away. Athletics serve the Black player well during his playing career, but does nothing to prepare the man for life after the glory. We find too many players ending up on drugs, divorced, broke, go to prison and even murder someone. Where was Tom Landry when Bob Hayes, one of the greatest wide receivers in Dallas, Cowboy history, needed a friend? Black players better wake up and understand that they are appreciated as long as they can effectively participate in a violent game. If there is a place where the old adage, "what have you done for me lately," is applicable it is in professional sports. With that in mind, the young player must begin to look to the future his very first year in the league. These young men fail to discern between what a hefty paycheck is and what wealth is. My point being when you are spending as much money as you are making, then you are not accumulating wealth. You don't measure wealth by the size of a paycheck, you measure it according to your assets. It is somewhat understandable when a young man, who comes from poverty, all of a sudden has millions of dollars and he fails to control his spending. However, at some point in his career, someone needs to counsel him on money management. His career lasts a very short time. More than likely, he still has more years to live after he retires, and therefore, must discipline and prepare for that time. If the young athlete, entering the league with energy and confidence, does not learn from the mistakes of players that have gone before him, then when it comes time for him to be turned out to pasture he will feel lifeless and defeated, a perfect formula for drugs, crime, and even death.

The Lemmings:

Too many young and gifted Black children are taking on the lemming effect when it comes to their future in sports. Lemmings are mouse like rodents. They are the smallest mammal in the Arctic Sea. Lemmings control the rhythm of animal life on the frozen tundra. They are an important food source for other Arctic animals. Lemmings remain active throughout the winter, they do not freeze to death, and they can reproduce within weeks.

Approximately every four years, in the spring, the lemmings migrate across the waters of the Arctic. They attempt to reach the other side of the sea. Thousands of lemmings die believing they can make it across the waters. Many lemmings have to die before that one lemming turns back and leads the rest to dry land. Today, we must be that one who turns back and leads our people to dry land. We need that one person who is willing to stop this rush to our own demise. We must turn back and take a new direction in our communities, schools, churches, mosques, spiritual centers and families. There has to be more men and women turning back to our natural God-given ability. We must give our energy and attention to our physical, mental, financial and spiritual needs. We need the entire Black race to make that turn today and not be like the lemmings that diligently try to cross that water, but ultimately self-destruct. Not every Black child will have blazing speed, be able to jump high, dunk a basketball, sing or dance. But many Black children will have the God-given ability to comprehend an algebra formula, learn more than one language, write a poem or novel, and understand Socrates and Satre. Sydney J. Harris wrote, "no single way of living is exclusively right." I agree because not every Black child is born to be an athlete. We have to become accountants, scientists, and most important teachers. We must become accountable to ourselves today. We accomplish that by expanding our horizons into areas that were unfamiliar to us in totality.

Black athletes, like the lemmings, control the rhythm of the sports industry. They are the source of tremendous wealth for the owners. Not only do they perform on the athletic fields, but they also serve a vital function in the communities that make them famous. They participate in charity events as a gesture to please the owners and the masses, while ignoring their own communities, or doing very little to bring about change in them. These athletes, however, never seem to recognize that they are dispensable. They are like economy cars.

When one goes down, owners can find hundreds just waiting to replace them. They come knocking at the owner's door, pleading for a chance to get into the arena and prove they are worthy of consideration. The supply is endless.

Perhaps the greatest amount of exploitation occurs within the college ranks. Colleges exploit athletes as if they were in a third world country sweatshop. College players should be paid for their services. The coaches get paid, the trainers get paid, the athletic director gets paid, and so should the player. When the young athlete's college career is over, they become like the lemmings trying to cross the arctic to find fame and fortune in the professional ranks. Only a very small percentage will make it. Thousands lose their self-esteem, self-worth, self-confidence, self-reliance, and die mentally trying so desperately to cross over. Many of them die spiritually because all of their hope was in a dream that someone else had created for them.

Just as lemmings tend to be more aggressive towards each other, athletes fit this same mode whenever their coaches wind them up just like a play toy. I am angered when I see Black high school, college and professional players fighting among themselves, like slaves on a plantation, even before the clock starts ticking. It is as if they are trying to show their master how much they love him. The love is so deep that they are willing to hurt their fellow brother, and sacrifice their own body just to get a pat on the back from the coach. There was a player, a great linebacker for the Pittsburg Steelers, who was ordered by the NFL to stay on his 30 yard line during pre-game exercises in a 2005 playoff game. The player had been talking "trash" to his opponents during the warm up session, and it had become unnerving. As the world watched the linebacker pace back and forth, he never crossed that line. His obedience was apparent as he waited for the sound of the master's whistle. He was waiting for his master to say "bite"! Without his uniform, without his master to let him out of his cage, this linebacker has no bite at all. There are millions of people sitting back and laughing at us when we behave in the manner of a contemporary American slave. As athletes we must always be aware of the steps we take, for fear of falling out of step and becoming a puppet for a system that cares very little about us as humans. We must overcome the lemming's effect and stop before we go so far that we cannot turn away from the madness of this world.

The Last Athlete:

The last athlete has been born and he is running without a sense of his history or a sense of consciousness. Only the orders from his coach are his blue print for a life of competition. He seeks accolades from his coach, praises that can be given to him and as easily taken away. The last athlete lives in an environment that he did not chose. You witness it everyday when a baby is born. Those around him and make comments, "he's so big, he's going to be a football player," or "he's going to be real tall just look at his feet," and "he's going to be so fast, he's going to run for his country in the Olympic Games." Today, however, the last athlete is running with a purpose. He realizes, at another time in America, he was not considered a person and was

143

subjected to the cruelty of slavery. He understands that slavery was a lie, and the institution of slavery violates the laws of humanity and civilization. The last athlete is running with a moral compass of absolutes that allow him to understand man's true nature. According to Albert Einstein, "the real problem is in the hearts and minds of men, it is not a problem of physics but of ethics. It is easier to denature plutonium than to denature the evil spirit of man." The last athlete understands that his people have been the pawns of an athletic mass deception, and it has control of the Black community. And like an atomic bomb, it has eradicated all value laden pursuits among our young. These values have been replaced with love for a violent game, like football. The reason Blacks in America love sports so much is because the world view demands it. We are to be at our best when we are in the athletic arena. The last athlete first began running when Charles W. Follis, the first Black professional football player, took to the field in 1902. He was given the nick name the Black Cyclone because of his supernatural speed at that time. It has been over 100 years since the Black Cyclone broke into professional sports in America, and now other Black Cyclones are still running in the Olympics, the NCAA, the NBA and in MLB. And the last athlete is especially running in the ultimate super power of sports, the NFL, where millions dream, thousands sacrifice, and only a few will benefit. You have to be tough to be a football player, but you have to be even tougher to tell people the truth about it all. (The last athlete is still running.)

Conclusion

Since 1946, the sporting establishment has controlled the lives of Black athletes. They control how we play and how we retire. They have projected their culture as the primary point of reference. This was easy to do considering they make the rules. Take away the dunk in basketball, eliminate the forward pass in football and you can eliminate the Black athlete. He will find himself in another Dark Age of sports. They have toyed with us, and humiliated us on a national level. They project us like trained monkeys in a cage. They leverage us with their money in exchange for our blood. It has been written that God saved Daniel from the lion's den. God saved Jonah from the belly of a giant fish. God saved the Hebrew children from the fiery furnace. God gave David the courage to fight Goliath. May God give favor to the Black athlete to stand today and save himself from athletic enslavement.

Chapter Ten

IN SEARCH OF A NEW HUMANITY

*In our search for God we have been given a theological
tradition that suffocates our spiritual instincts— AP*

A person without a dream will spend his entire life littering the landscape and wondering why. There are people in certain positions in life, some in leadership roles and others following the rulers. I was a back up to pro bowlers in the NFL. I have played suited up with hall of famers, and today I am their voice. They are reading my books and reciting my words.

When the universe was created, the God of all had a solo performance. His was the greatest feat of all time. However God has instructed His prophets, Buddha, Muhammad, and Jesus to conduct performances of greatness in His name. The greatest of all those acts was Jesus Christ rising from death and two thousand years later we are still celebration that event. Athletes in team sports also engage in solo performances, and that is why leagues give solo awards, such as Most Valuable Player, Outstanding Player, and Pro Bowl Invitations. ESPN also gives individual awards for solo performances. Don't be deceived by a coach saying "be a team player." How can I be a team player when the team and league give awards for individual achievements?

Sports and The Human Spirit:

Religion was never meant to be a tool to solve the problems of humanity. It takes human beings to fix problems within the human race. Think of all the innocent human beings that have survived so much injustice, none of which can be justified in the eyes of man and God. Races have used faulty reasoning to justify their acts against other races of people. Europeans argued that they were justified when they went into Africa and stole millions of people, brought them to a strange land and kept them in bondage. Their reasoning being that the people they placed in bondage were less than human beings. Enslaving and introducing them to western civilization was a benevolent act. Early Americans, who are merely an extension of Europeans, used the same kind of convoluted logic while terrorizing and slaughtering the Indians. Under the edict of "Manifest Destiny," and the "White Man's Burden", they declared the Indians as uncivilized and it was their God given duty to take the land for civilized people. In a recent article, the former chief of an Alaskan tribe criticized the Republican vice presidential candidate because of her complicity in an on-going policy of ignoring the rights of the original people in that state. He claimed that ever since the original Treaty of Cession in 1867 that sold Alaska to the United States the treatment towards Alaskan Native people has been fairly consistent. They, as were Africans and Native Americans, referred to as less than human,

147

"uncivilized tribes", so they were excluded from any dialogues and decisions regarding the land they had occupied for generations. They fell victim to the dominating "Manifest Destiny" myth that God had given Americans their land to take from them because they were non-Christians and incapable of self-government. This former chief clearly accuses the American government and its people of a vile violation of their human rights. So European-Americans not only stole from the African and Indian, their natural spirituality and forced on them Christianity with all its evil to include slavery, massacre, Jim Crow, lynching, the KKK and contemporary sports, but also are still stealing from the Alaskan natives under the leadership of the present governor.

Today, many of us who have been victims of this false doctrine have suffered self-destruction in our beliefs, our thinking, and our confidence. We must begin to recognize the falsehoods involved in early European American propaganda. We have to spend time seeking spiritual truths in order to reconnect with the God within us. Seeking truth is equivalent to building physical muscles. The more you bring blood into the tissue, the stronger the muscle will develop into a powerful force. The more we practice our spiritual gifts, the lies that have been perpetuated against God will have no influence on our being. When you begin changing the way you think about your importance to the world, everything in your life will begin to change also.

One might conclude that I emphasize the negative forces at work in our world too much and at the expense of those positive events that happen all around us. I do recognize the hand of God at work in nature and in the kind deeds that many of my fellow human beings perform. There are good people who see beyond the materialism, the greed, and the garbage that often dominates our society. But it is not the positive attributes that need to be addressed, although we must acknowledge they exist, it is the negative forces that threaten to destroy our existence if not put in check. Every great world empire has come to ruin because of one simple fact and that is the people became apathetic and distant themselves from the God within. Society loses its spirituality because the people get fed the worst kind of theological doctrine. They replace the God within themselves with institutionalized religion, manifested in churches, and ministers who give them concepts of God that are faulty and misleading. At times we are all aware of the pathologies around us. Considering all the evil that saturates our eyes and ears, you would think we should have destroyed ourselves long ago. The fact that we haven't is a strong indicator that good within still outweighs evil intentions. Jesus is symbolic of the good, and his resurrection proof that evil will lose this battle for our souls if we only learn to believe and trust in the God within ourselves. Jesus' message to us was not to follow Him the person, but His teachings which come directly from God. In Hebrews 8:10, God tells us, "For this is the covenant that I will make with the house of Israel after those days. I will put my laws in their mind and write them on their hearts, and I will be their God, and they shall be my people." The Israel that God is speaking of is not a geographical location. The house of Israel is the human body, the temple that houses the spirit of God, the spirit that never dies. The laws represent the true nature of mans, mind, spirit and intellect. The heart represents the foresight to make sound decisions that will impact your life. The heart never makes hasty decisions. We must all understand that our emotions dwell in our stomach and our knowledge sits in our brain. They both meet at the heart where sound decisions are made that affect our future in a positive and sound way. When making decisions solely on emotions without facts, our life gets out of balance. We end up getting divorced and changing careers many times. Our friends seem to come and go along with our health.

That kind of suffering is not the way to grow closer to God. Why would God create a beautiful earth, with all of nature's essence, only to create human beings to war among themselves? God has given us a wonderful palace with trees, oceans, mountains and valleys then we turn around and destroy it in many different ways. It is like a mother preparing the baby's room with beautiful colors, artwork on the walls, and when the baby arrives she places him or her in the crib and proceeds to burn down the house. God wouldn't do that and it makes no sense when we, as human beings, do just that. What makes tremendous sense is Matthew 6:33, "but seek first the kingdom of God, all his righteousness, and all these things shall be added to you." The very same power, essence, deity, God and spirit that raised Jesus from the dead, I can also call upon to move things in my life, to help me reach the pinnacle in my quest for higher understanding. This power gives us assurance that the spirit is alive today and available to those willing to think like God. If you want to emulate Christ, you have to be willing to think like Him, a conqueror, a king, a believer, and a God. You have to acquire the mental capacity to see your success before you achieve it. This gives the performer the ability to eliminate fear, doubt, and uncertainty. The path you travel today must be filled with steps of confidence. There has to be foresight, insight, and vision. If not, you are going down a road that "never was."

Never Was:

Assisting a young man in his pursuit of a professional career, in any sport, is filled with ups and downs, tragedies, triumphs, losses, along with championships. I have always been torn between my love of football and my devotion to my own spirituality. Football and spirituality have nothing in common. Football is a game with a beginning and ending, it has rules, regulations and boundaries. It is a game sanctioned by the rich men that have control over its very existence. The game gives nothing to the human soul, rather lends itself to the complete destruction of the human body. It is a finite game that young men, facing a life of poverty, gravitate toward and look at as their only hope for survival. They become beholden to the rich, who are the owners of the franchises of violence.

Spirituality is a way of life that has no ending, but rather continues on infinitely. The game of spirituality purifies the mind, body and soul, this trinity has been in unison together since the dawn of civilization. Until man fully connects with his spirituality, he will continue chasing a future that never was.

I believe in chasing the dream, and also going after the desires of the heart. But I advocate that individuals know the odds so they can successfully navigate through the mire that often cripples the will of the individual. When young men are not exposed to the truth or refuse to acknowledge the reality of life all around them, they may well be living a life that "never was." There has to be a spiritual base in the young athlete's life in order to give him direction. The individual that chases the dream and knows the odds are against him, but holds onto the humanness within will be victorious. However in today's world, we are witnessing our fellow human beings losing this special quality when life challenges them. They fail to realize their dream can come to an abrupt end, a result that is out of their control. When young men are chasing an athletic dream they are putting their career in the hands of strangers who will only give them an opportunity to succeed, and not a guarantee.

The majority of athletes making the transition from high school to college then to the pros always say the same thing, "all I'm looking for is an opportunity." These are not the words of power, rather words of uncertainty. You cannot visualize success based on an opportunity. We have to call things forth in our life and make them happen, just as Jesus called Lazareth forth from the dead. We must call on the God within ourselves to change our lives, because too many of us are dead concerning the tree of knowledge.

Athletics and life are not on the same plateau with each other. They are not parallel pursuits but in fact differ in many ways. Life is in harmony with nature. It is a cycle of rules that never come into conflict with each other. One may think hurricanes and tornados are a conflict of nature, to the contrary, it is the cleansing of itself. Athletics is a competition that breeds evil characteristics such as envy, jealousy, and misplaced pride. In athletics, you do not grow intellectually, in actuality you gradually decline physically. The same physical drills you do in middle school to improve your athletic ability, you do in high school, college, and in the pros. To maintain a slave being a slave, eliminate education from him.

With our intellectual pursuits, we arrive at a point of maturity and gain knowledge and wisdom. With athletics, we wake up with broken bones, lost dreams, shattered self-confidence, and shattered emotions. This happens when we spend so much valuable time building physical muscles that have a limited window of professional performance. Rather the development of the mind and intellect which can perform throughout an entire life time. The Good Book says, "The mind is strong, but the body is weak". If we live wrapped in the shallowness of football, we will stay a child always being told what to do, how to do it, and when to do it. In that condition we will live a life that never was.

Humanness:

I believe that we, as a society, have forgotten what it means to be humane. For centuries humans have called on religion to solve the problems of greed, racism, sexism, and all other un-civilized behavior. We have pretty much taken God out of our daily lives, calling on Him only in times of crisis. The American populace, as members of the human race, operates from a center of selfishness, where personal gain is the religion of the day. The love of God is often replaced for the love of money and materialism. It was not meant to be like this, mass confusion about what it means to be a good person. Individuals are scrambling to find new religions, practices, and beliefs in their desperate attempt to connect again with God. But the God you are looking for is right here with you reading this book. When a community is disconnected from God, it shows in their culture, the character of the people and the chaos and confusion in the streets. We must humanize ourselves once again, make ourselves humane, kind, merciful, civilized, refined, and most of all love one another. These are the attributes of Jesus. He operated within the human spirit. Jesus went to the cross to affirm the power of the human spirit, mind, and consciousness. His death that Friday on the cross symbolizes our burdens. There is a cross we all have to bear, the cross of our minds, thoughts, and twisted beliefs. We need to take these false concepts of God and let them die also on the cross, and allow the righteousness of the human spirit to be raised back up in us. God is never outside of us, but the spirit of God dwells deep inside of our existence. It is unfortunate that our spirituality is absent from our body. It happened when we took God out of everything and placed Him somewhere in outer space. That is why it is so easy for man to slowly destroy the earth. We have Al Gore, bless his being, telling the world to make peace with the earth, when as dehumanized beings we cannot make peace with ourselves. It is not my responsibility to judge how we live, it is my job to help us understand why we live a godless life within this godless society.

For centuries America was a godless country because it took men and women out of their native land, in the most inhumane way ever committed against another people, and placed them in slavery. There is no justification for the enslavement of any human beings, and if a religion argues it is all right, those in charge of that religion must be put on trial in the world court of justice. I believe that any religion that supported slavery should be put on trial. Realize that during slavery the profiteers were not only the plantation owners. Every corner of the world made a profit; some are still living off the interest their ancestors accrued and past on through generations. It is called inheritance. In *Genesis, 1:26* "God said let us make men in our image, in our likeness and man shall rule over the fish of the sea and the birds of the air, over the livestock, over all the earth and over all the creatures that move along the ground." God never told us to make slaves out of other men made in his image. The only person to make a slave is a human being who has been dehumanized.

Valid measures give accurate conclusions—A.P

T-Boone Pickens, who is a great business man, said that the largest transfer of wealth in the history of the world is taking place right before our eyes. However, I would suggest that the largest transfer of wealth in the world was the transporting of Africans to America during the Trans Atlantic slave trade. To this day, it is the worst crime of all centuries. The cruelty was unimaginable, the profits inconceivable, and the benefactors still collecting interest after all these years through inheritance. The slave trade established a historically unique relationship between five distinct entities; 1) Anglos, 2) Africans, 3) the Atlantic Ocean, 4) America, and 5) Athletes. This relationship works as follows; the Anglo opened up the Atlantic Ocean to slave ships with human cargo from Africa, and eventually turned the cotton fields into football fields and made athletes.

We can also examine this relationship from a numerical perspective. There are 53 countries in Africa, and between the years 1444 and 1888 there were 53,000 slave voyages from Africa to the Americas. There was a slave rebellion on the slave ship Amistad on July 2, 1839, off the east coast of the United States. There were 53 slaves on that ship. In the NFL each team has a 53 man roster. Africa has the largest reserve of natural resources in the world, yet has the poorest people. America is the richest country in the world, and it produces the greatest athletes from the poorest neighborhoods. The slave ships, Africa, and athletes all represent private property, profit and wealth. There were dogs imported from Cuba to America to hunt down run away slaves. These dogs were named "nigger hunters." From the time they were puppies the "nigger hunters" were trained to catch runaways. Even to this day when you call Cuba, you have to dial 53 for the international line. Spain had its 311, America had its 911 and every year I have my 53. I reflect on those 53,000 voyages and pray for the souls lost in the Atlantic Ocean. I reflect on the thousands of babies in their mother's womb, born into slavery and died in slavery, never experiencing freedom. America committed a crime against humanity and it still remains to be brought into balance with universal Karma.

"The best knowledge is personal knowledge. Book knowledge is written by authors who seldom have the experience of what they write about."—A.P

Conclusion:

I write about my experiences in a way to make my reader question the things they accept as truth. It is very important that I succeed in spreading my message about sports and spirituality. We must always super charge the human spirit. It was important to the success of Frederick Douglass, Booker T. Washington, and it is now important to Anthony E. Prior. There comes a moment in life when the world is going to need your solo performance, whether a professional dancer performing in front of thousands and bringing the audience to tears with effortless motion, or a roaring speech that sparks new emotions in people to start living better lives, or a teacher in a run down public school with apathetic children changing the students' lives by first changing herself. I must win this game because the game of life does not stop, only the human heart. Almost is not good enough today. We have to finish all our tasks we start. We must see our dreams come into fruition. Success has to be lived, shared, and celebrated today. If not, what is this life all about? Imagine putting everything into something and get nothing. That would be devastating to the human psyche and could kill the mightiest of men.

As long as people continue to believe that God exists outside of them, they will continue to suffer from confusion. I remember during my professional football career, players would always function between God-Jesus-the Holy Ghost-Spirit and football. During Bible study the preacher would talk about world suffering, the lack of resources plaguing countries around the world. In an attempt to solicit money from them, he talked directly to their emotions. He looked directly into my eyes, but quickly looked away. He could sense that my intellect was not controlled by emotions and I saw right through his con game. I don't mean to imply that all ministers are con artists. But there are definitely large contingents who seek their own personal gain at the expense of all other considerations. Even more amazing was the number of players who pulled out their check books and wrote checks, ranging from five to fifteen thousand dollars, to a man and a ministry they hadn't taken time to investigate. These same athletes come from communities where that kind of money is in great need. These players should be donating resources to those children who are much like they were before entering the lucrative sports industry. Every professional athlete should hold on to what is considered money for tithes until after the season, then visit children that will be directly affected in a positive way by their contribution and will, parenthetically, appreciate it much more than the hustling minister. I refer to them as hustlers because often they will not show up to the facility after a loss on that Sunday before payday. When players lose it is difficult to touch their emotions in a way that they are willing to give. It is only after a victory, when that victory can be explained as the work of God and therefore, they must give back to him by giving the minister a hefty check. It is called "Religious manipulation."

158

BLACK HORSES/WHITE COTTON AND RELIGION

1. Get what you want from others when others are not willing initially to give

2. Con people to worship what you want them to believe in

3. Present reality the way you want players to see it rather than the way it really is

4. Get others to feel like they are responsible for your well-being

Religion has divided this world into warring camps because of the ignorance involved with most religious teachings. If your religion does not allow you to search for the truth, that is no religions at all. You are in what I call a religious enslavement. I once had a discussion with a colleague, and when he saw I was reading a book about a philosopher named Rene Descartes, who claimed "I think, therefore, I am," in 1644, he scowled at me and shouted I was going to hell because I was gravitating towards spiritual fulfillment outside the Bible. According to his limited thinking, our college education should be based only on one book. Imagine how much knowledge would be lost under that kind of arrangement. Imagine only being allowed to travel in one direction. If your mind cannot expand, neither can your life. If the world cannot balance itself with truth, fairness, justice, equality, and freedom, what do we have to look forward to in the future?

The individual is primarily responsible for is "self". It is vital that I take care of Anthony Prior mentally, physically, financially, and spiritually. If not, then I am not good for anyone else. You can not wait for things to happen for you. It is important that you be the trend setter starting today, and take that leap to become what you were meant to be, not something others have made you. If you can sit in a quiet room and visualize your success, then you can live that reality if you get up and get going. Have you ever listened to the same song over and over again, and each time you heard the song, it was as if you heard it for the first time. That is a great feeling. Now imagine having that feeling for a life time. That's what life is, you either run or dance through it with a rhythm all your own. You do not need religion, or theological doctrines to go to Heaven, you can't buy your way in either. Heaven is a way of life, it is how you eat, live, and communicate with your surroundings. Man and woman have lost their way and no longer follow the teachings in the Old and New Testament. Contemporary society has pushed God away and decided to remove Him from our daily lives. It all started with the banning of prayer in schools. Without prayer in any part of our lives leads to chaos. What we have today is a very chaotic society, including the vicious activities that take place on the football field, to feed the vicious and blood thirsty nature of the spectators. The Super Bowl is the most watched sporting event of the year, and one of the most watched events of all televised programs. Football is symptomatic of what is wrong with our society today. We have lost our way and no longer put our faith in each other.

When people can't see a future for themselves, they anticipate the worst of what life has to offer, and that is exactly what they attract into their lives. They are surrounded by the ills of society and experience a "spiritual ghetto." However, give a person a road map filled with truth, love, and understanding and it will ultimately lead them to their freedom. Freedom is the sum total of God. Understand that freedom does not just descend upon the individual; he/she must raise themselves to the level of freedom. *Ezra 9 vs. 9* tells us, "we were slaves yet our God did not forsake us in bandage, but He extended mercy to us in the sight of the Kings of Persia to revive us to repair the house of our God to rebuild its ruins and to give us a wall in Judah and Jerusalem." Today, we need spiritual freedom and a path to reconnect to the human spirit. We are no longer enslaved to dogma, but have come to a point in our lives where we understand the same old religion that didn't fix the past and can't fix the troubled future. We must repair the house of God mentally, physically, and spiritually and live in a manner free from religious bigotry of any kind. Build walls around your mind engraved with the truth. Know you have the power of God within to protect you from religious lies that have kept you in the dark, and living a life of mediocrity.

We can all get satisfaction from the truth that the mind of Jesus will be back again. This time He is coming back with justice, love, and eternal salvation for the soul of those who care to follow His teachings that come directly from God. There is a new world coming, led by the greatest prophet of them all Jesus. In this new beginning the world will experience freedom to connect with God the Supreme Being. The same mind power Jesus tapped into you can as well. Change your life and put the God in you back into the driver' seat.

A FINAL MESSAGE: EIGHTY-ONE APISMS

1. If you wait for anything in this lifetime you will wait forever.—AP

2. To be ready for it , first master it.—AP

3. Every problem we encounter the answers are in nature.—AP

4. If religion can give you a better life, then I'm all for that.—AP

5. Do you know about Fort Jesus in Africa?—AP

6. A coach can take away a scholarship from you without threatening you, all he needs is a woman's lying tongue.—AP

7. The weak always wants to interrupt the life of the strong, with jail.—AP

8. Goals are the driving force behind motivation.—AP

9. An athlete can only take you where he is, and that only subjects you to a physical battle. An athlete can not take you to Heaven if he is running in hell.—AP

10. You can go through something and not become

it.—AP

11. I would rather see the actions of a great sermon than hearing one.—AP

12. The owners, his president, and the coaches sell one thing-pain.—AP

13. We spend so much time praying to God for things we were never meant to have.—AP

14. The sports industry has you spilling your own blood.—AP

15. There are no happy endings when you decide to leave sports.—AP

16. No other sport in the world reveals the character of a man more than American football.—AP

17. The New Testament cannot stand without the Old Testament. The new Black athlete cannot stand without the once condemned n----r.—AP

18. When the lights of sports go out we are not going to reflect on the coach's words, nor condemn his actions, we are going to condemn our silence.—AP

19. This book is about the future and the past and how they come together.—AP

20. The new limbs on a tree can not stand without old

roots.—AP

21. The 21st Century masters could not stand without the 21st Century slaves of today.—AP

22. What makes one man better than the other; exposure.—AP

23. An athlete should always give knowledge and perceptive, not only about sports, but also about life.—AP

24. Who is stopping it from happening?—AP

25. Change only happens in people when they start living again.—AP

26. There is no past, no present, no future; it is all in the wind.—AP

27. The human has a linear concept, but the spirit is timeless.—AP

28. I speak to teach and I write to convict.—AP

29. Keep a good thing going.—AP

30. When you are angry from the words of a friend, take away the words and then re-evaluate the situation.—AP

31. People cry when they get what they wish for.—AP

32. Pro athletes are on an entirely different level, they are worshipped.—AP

33. Fans and spectators cannot see racism because they are standing in the way.—AP

34. The athlete can only be in the moment.—AP

35. The future is based on motion.—AP

36. There is no future in loving a slave or an athlete, they can only be loved by the extension of their master's hand.—AP

37. I know how to reach players because I have been a player myself.—AP

38. You do not look for freedom, it is something you experience.—AP

39. You have to write it the way you envision it.—AP

40. What good is religion if you remain the same?—AP

41. What good is a degree if it does not give you an independent mind?—AP

42. What good is a friend if he does not challenge your ignorance?—AP

43. People will value you when you can do something for them.—AP

44. Football is an unhealthy activity.—AP

45. You can not pray and stand still.—AP

46. Ghetto means you do not own anything.—AP

47. God calls you for the future.—AP

48. Understand these so-called great coaches, with their championships; their success is in you.—AP

49. When you start with peace, it will end peacefully.—AP

50. There was a double slavery, physical slavery and \ mental slavery.—AP

51. Today we are crippled by our culture.—AP

52. Remember the lie will continue to change.—AP

53. Run hard, read hard, write hard, pray hard, and speak harder.—AP

54. Sports needs to be outlawed for ten years in the black community, a grace period to reconnect to what we originally set out to accomplish.—AP

55. The freedom you desire is within.—AP

56. When is the last time you allowed God to entertain you.—AP

57. When one in an oppressed race finds success in the hands of his oppressor, he see no oppression at all.—AP

58. Every time a Black athlete elevates his level of competition he is born again.—AP

59. You become enlightened when you open your third eye.—AP

60. God does not make pro athletes, men do. God does not make slaves, men do.—AP

61. They gathered a few, which turned into hundreds, then thousands, which grew to millions and they sold them.—AP

62. Athletes are created.—AP

63. The very thing that has made the Black athlete good is running him down today.—AP

64. The two industries that have destroyed the Black

community are slavery and the pursuit of sports.—
AP

65. Most people want to be tall like trees, so others will look up to them.—AP

66. To have power is the means of control, to love is to understand peace.—AP

67. How do you suppress people, keep them young of mind.—AP

68. When you are a grown man playing a kids game, you never grow up.—AP

69. No coach can hinder me.—AP

70. Horses like slaves must earn their way to Heaven, unlike white cotton it sits in the Heavens like clouds in the sky.—AP

71. A person's skin is soft because they have not experienced hardship.—AP

72. Everybody's agenda is different.—AP

73. There is always one amongst the crowd that has a message.—AP

74. They are cheering you on, louder than ever before in history, because they are almost done with you.—AP

75. The coaches look for a player with a rage within himself, one he cannot explain and one a coach can control.—AP

76. A player who knows his value is more dangerous to management than his opponent.—AP

77. Team sports have to be integrated to allow the presence of the weaker athlete.—AP

78. They put you in the hunt like a dog for a championship.—AP

79. They never tell you why.—AP

80. There is a n----r list in pro sports, and I've read it.—AP

81. I am an eyewitness to the biggest conspiracy in the 21st Century concerning African Americans. Sports can save you from a life of hardship.—AP

Made in the USA
Columbia, SC
26 November 2022

72098340R00109